PERFECT CURTAINS

PERFECT
CURTAINS

SMART AND SIMPLE SOLUTIONS
USING FABULOUS FABRICS

jacqui
small

Stephanie Hoppen

PHOTOGRAPHY BY SIMON UPTON

First published in 2009 by Jacqui Small LLP,
an imprint of Aurum Press Ltd
7 Greenland Street
London NW1 0ND

PUBLISHER Jacqui Small
EDITORIAL MANAGER Lesley Felce
PROJECT EDITOR AND WRITER Zia Mattocks
ART DIRECTOR Sarah Rock
SWATCH PHOTOGRAPHY Deirdre Rooney
SWATCH STYLIST Alison Davidson
ADDITIONAL PHOTOGRAPHY Greg Cox
PRODUCTION Peter Colley

ISBN: 978 1 906417 10 9

2011 2010 2009
10 9 8 7 6 5 4 3 2 1
Printed in Singapore

PAGE 1: The colour scheme
for this guest bedroom was
designed by Jackye Lanham
to tie in with the floral fabric
used for the pretty curtains with
pleated and buttoned headings.

PAGES 2–3: Pollack's Gloss
fabric has been used to make
these stunning semi-sheer
curtains in an Atlanta living
room designed by Tim Hobby, of
interior design showroom Space.

PAGE 4: A wonderful decorative
sheer – Freshness in the colour
Earth – designed by Larry Laslo
for Robert Allen, and used for a
stunning bed curtain in Laslo's
New York home.

PAGE 5: In a room designed by
Kelly Hoppen, parachute silk has
been generously layered over a
Silent Gliss blind that prevents
the bright light from streaming
into the interior.

Contents

Introduction

THERE HAVE BEEN REMARKABLE CHANGES IN THE WORLD OF INTERIOR DESIGN OVER THE PAST DECADE — AND IT IS A SEEMINGLY EVER-CHANGING AREA. AT ONE STAGE, THE PENDULUM SWUNG SO FAR INTO THE MINIMALIST STYLE THAT EVEN A BOOK PLACED ON A COFFEE TABLE MIGHT BE CONSIDERED TO RUIN THE EFFECT. ACHIEVING PERFECT MINIMALISM IS A VERY DIFFICULT TASK, AND FOR MOST OF US IT IS NOT A STYLE IN WHICH WE FIND MUCH COMFORT. I KNOW THAT EVENTUALLY THE PENDULUM WILL SWING DECIDEDLY IN THE OTHER DIRECTION, AND BAROQUE WILL BE BACK WITH A VENGEANCE — I RATHER HOPE I'LL BE AROUND TO SEE WHAT FORM THIS TAKES. THERE ARE ALREADY SIGNS OF IT IN FABRICS, AND LITTLE TOUCHES HERE AND THERE IN OTHERWISE VERY MODERN ROOMS.

Nothing about our way of decorating our homes, however, has changed as much as the way in which we treat our windows – be it with curtains, blinds, shutters, screens or nothing at all. There has been a significant sea change over the past few years, from formal to informal, from heavy to light, from lined and interlined to unlined and free-floating, from valances and French pleats to more relaxed interpretations of traditional heading styles – but, most of all, it is now all about the fabric. There is a vast choice with not many rules – and the remaining rules are to do with what is left out, rather than what is included. The results are wonderful. Curtains have become freer, lighter, multifunctional and – dare I say it – fun.

Curtains are an expense, and mistakes must be avoided, so I hope that the following chapters will help to inform, inspire and guide you through the many options available and enable you make the right choices for your home. There are some stunning examples of curtains in all sorts of fabrics and styles – from sheer voile to heavy linen, glamorous silk to luxurious cashmere, relaxed checks and smart stripes to pretty florals – designed by leading interior designers and made by expert curtain makers, photographed in homes around the world. I believe that a picture is worth a thousand words. Simply being able to say to your curtain maker, 'That is what I am looking for,' makes this book worthwhile.

LEFT: Embroidery can give a wonderful couture touch to any fabric, from pretty sheers to heavier cottons and linens. The tone-on-tone geometric design on this Mahe fabric from Sahco introduces pattern into a room in a subtle way, while the contrast between the silky embroidery threads and the background linen provides a great textural element.

OPPOSITE: This suite of rooms in La Residence in Franschhoek, one of the most exquisite regions of South Africa's Cape, has golden tangerine pure silk curtains hanging abundantly and luxuriously from a simple iron pole. The curtains are lined and have blackout under-curtains. Showcasing the silk against this type of pole is so chic. Pure silk, when hung in this seemingly unceremonious way, is the ultimate in glamour, and it is interesting to note how the straightforward way in which the curtains are hung fits so seamlessly into a room filled with fine objects and furniture and a wonderfully ornate Indian chandelier.

Let the fabric do the talking

AS WE PHOTOGRAPHED HOMES ALL OVER THE UNITED STATES, THE UK, FRANCE AND SOUTH AFRICA, EVERY INTERIOR DESIGNER, FABRIC DESIGNER AND CURTAIN MAKER THAT I INTERVIEWED HAD THE SAME MANTRA. IT IS THE AMAZING CHOICE OF FABRICS THAT WE HAVE AVAILABLE TO US NOW — IN NEW DESIGNS, COLOURS AND DIFFERENT WEIGHTS — THAT HAS DICTATED THIS SHIFT TO SIMPLICITY, TO LETTING THE FABRICS THEMSELVES TAKE CENTRE STAGE.

Doreen Scott, soft furnishings producer for many leading interior designers, including Kelly Hoppen, Anoushka Hempel and Mimmi O'Connell, brings to her draperies, windows and upholstery a theatrical imagination, together with great practicality and an extraordinary simplicity and vision. Doreen agreed that the biggest and most dramatic change in draperies and their treatment is, without doubt, due to the current availability and wide choice of extraordinary and beautiful fabrics that simply did not exist even as little as five years ago. In particular, there is a bewilderingly large choice of linens and sheers in every weight, pattern and colour. I was also astonished to find fabrics that can be ordered to an exact recipe – hand-painted, if necessary, and in any colour in the spectrum. Fabrics that we never dreamed of a few years ago are suddenly everywhere, and are leading the way towards a totally new and exciting look.

The other important factor in the new approach to curtains is the understanding that linings and interlinings often restrict the way the fabric would fall naturally and can, therefore, destroy the sensuality of a great fabric. Designers are now frequently leaving curtains unlined in favour of layering, as they prefer the way the fabric hangs

OPPOSITE LEFT: Liz Biden has given a pure blue silk taffeta a tightly pleated border that in turn is topped with another frilled border of blue-and-cream checked silk. It is the mixture of these two fabrics – the almost gingham effect against the glamorous plain silk taffeta – that makes the curtain so interesting.

OPPOSITE RIGHT: Colour and pattern have been used to dramatic effect by American-born designer Hilton McConnico for adjacent panels of fabric on the window of this Paris home. The contrast between the striking black-and-white zebra stripe and the bold egg-yolk yellow makes for an arresting effect.

THIS PAGE: In a suite at La Residence, Liz Biden and Ralph Krall used lime green silk for the body of the curtains and mint green silk for the border, which has been pleated all the way to the bottom to give the curtains weight. The pink velvet daybed throws the curtains and room into focus.

when it is unlined. The fabrics themselves are superb, but the styling and workmanship of the new simple curtains are equally of the highest order, and these factors are what elevate a simple look to the realm of stunning.

It is fascinating to see how the approach to curtains has evolved. New York-based designer Vicente Wolf's timeless style has not changed dramatically since we last worked together – his understated elegance can never be anything but perfect. In the case of Jackye Lanham of Atlanta, there is a difference of emphasis, as well as a looser, less structured look. Jill Vantosh, also of Atlanta, has designed new ways to use white sheers, while Larry Laslo of New York has gone so far as to design an entire collection of sheer fabrics that are quite different to anything seen before and which are magical in creating new looks. Tim Hobby, of Space in Atlanta, has used screens of all sorts to cover windows, and this is something we saw and heard about worldwide – designers John Barman in New York and Mimmi O'Connell and Doreen Scott in London all felt that, in the right circumstances, screens can be a perfect way to cover windows instead of curtains or blinds.

With fabrics of every type now available in profusion, it is almost too difficult to choose. Doreen Scott's advice is to keep curtains timeless by avoiding pattern, unless it is tone-on-tone such as damask or a very subtle self-colour embroidery. Mimmi O'Connell favours linen and scrim, with ticking and vintage fabrics thrown into the mix. Whatever you select, when you find a fabric you desire, do not overwhelm it with linings and heavy pelmets and poles – let it dance for you.

LEFT: Bernie de Le Cuona has a unique style, evident both in the design of her wonderful range of fabrics and in the ways in which she uses them. Here, she has created drama and interest by lining a pure wool fabric called Duchess Paisley in Quirky with Washed Linen Plain Blueberry – a stunning contrast in texture, weight and style.

OPPOSITE TOP RIGHT: This delicate pattern called Willow, designed by Albert Hadley of the great Parish-Hadley of New York, has been custom-printed for interior designer Jonathan Reed in an ebony brown on an off-white ground. Monochromatic patterns are striking yet easy to live with, and these neutral colours will work well in most interior settings.

OPPOSITE TOP LEFT, BOTTOM LEFT AND BOTTOM RIGHT: While looking for exciting and colourful wool fabrics, I stumbled upon the wonderful world of Coral Stephens, a company in Swaziland that makes fabrics and curtains strictly to order for discerning clients all over the world. The company owns the goats, weaves the yarn and dyes the colours once the pattern and design have been decided on.

ABOVE LEFT: Any atmosphere can be created by the correct choice of fabric and design. Denise Bazzurro made these wool drapes for designer Tim Hobby, for the library of a house in Atlanta, Georgia. A wide trim at chair height, rather than at the bottom or top of a curtain, is an unusual touch. The drapes add gravitas to the library, in contrast to the other rooms in the house, which are filled with filmy white sheers.

ABOVE: Decorative sheers create wonderful plays of light and shadow when light shines through them. This example, which has frayed strips appliquéd onto a plain background, is called Timberland and is one of the new range designed by Larry Laslo for Robert Allen. The border is called Natures Web.

LEFT: I wanted a bedroom blind that would cut out most of the light at night, one that was feminine and soft, rather than sharp-edged, and I wanted a special fabric. This semi-sheer with fossilized leaves between the layers is from Andrew Martin's Friday Collection, called PLP01. Doreen Scott found a way to construct the blind so that no underpinnings are visible, even though the fabric is so soft and semi-sheer.

ABOVE: Bernie de Le Cuona has achieved a dramatic look by layering two stunning fabrics together, instead of using a fabric and lining. A stone-coloured linen with crewel embroidery called Sienna Stone has been paired with heavy 100 per cent linen hopsack, called Desert Cloth Brown – it looks amazing.

ABOVE RIGHT: Christina Strutt of Cabbages & Roses designs fabrics based on archive prints. The results are calming, restful and easy to live with. Tulips and Roses is a soft faded floral that works well in both traditional and contemporary interiors.

RIGHT: For the annual Kips Bay Decorator Show House 2008, Larry Laslo juxtaposed an ikat-design fabric with a die-cut semi-sheer for a very dramatic window treatment. The ikat pattern, Quintessence, in the colour Tourmaline, has been used on the walls, too, and is what creates the atmosphere of the bedroom.

BELOW: Doreen Scott created a soft, unstructured blind for my bathroom. It is easy to operate, the folds are feminine, and the pattern of the Dominique Kieffer white linen paisley fabric shows to perfection.

Design ideas

WINDOWS OF DIFFERENT SIZES AND SHAPES CAN
PRESENT DIFFICULTIES WHEN IT COMES TO DECIDING
ON A WINDOW TREATMENT. HOMES WITH VERY TALL
WINDOWS, FRENCH DOORS THAT OPEN INWARDS, AND
LARGE WINDOWS IN BEDROOMS THAT NEED TO HAVE A
ROOM-DARKENING TREATMENT ALL PRESENT UNIQUE
PROBLEMS. URBAN TOWERS WITH WALLS OF GLASS
NEED WINDOW TREATMENTS THAT OFFER PRIVACY AS
WELL AS SUN PROTECTION. GENERALLY, THIS REQUIRES
MOTORIZATION, WHICH IS A MAJOR CHANGE IN THE
INDUSTRY AND NEEDS THE INPUT OF AN ELECTRICIAN.

Window treatments can be used to alter a window's
dimensions. American designer Michael Tavano advises,
'My golden rule is to treat each window individually.
Dressing a window is the same as dressing a person –
identify and enhance the positives, and disguise the
negatives.' If a window has a great view but is very
narrow, you can extend the treatment on either side
and create the illusion of a bigger window. If you have
a wide, squat window with a tall ceiling, raise the rod
as high as possible, and hang a blind behind it. Pull
the blind down to where it breaks into the first pane of
glass, thereby tricking the eye and making the window
and the room seem taller. Pelmets and valances can
also be useful devices for creating an illusion of height.
Jackye Lanham created a false pelmet in duck-egg blue
above a low window in the kitchen of a seaside home,
with a natural-fibre blind beneath it (see page 21).

In an interior that has windows and French doors
of different shapes and sizes, curtains can be used to
unify the space and create an illusion of balance and
symmetry. In a house on Sea Island, Georgia (see right),

RIGHT: Curtains hanging simply from a narrow iron pole are
elegant, uncluttered, unfussy and all about the fabric. Here, Jackye
Lanham has used a semi-sheer cream-and-cinnamon checked fabric
for the curtains in this large living area in a house on Sea Island,
Georgia. Keeping the curtain rods at the same height all the way
around the room, even when the window heights and spaces are
different, creates a calm, balanced and peaceful environment.

BELOW: A symphony in black and white has been created by Jackye Lanham of Atlanta in the living area of her beach home in North Florida. Simple white curtains hang from the ubiquitous narrow iron poles that I love so much. The curtains are made from cotton seersucker, the perfect fabric for a seaside home where informality and comfort go hand in hand with Lanham's exquisite sense of style and hospitality. The black furniture gives the dining area definition.

OPPOSITE: In an ingenious use of fabric, interior designer Melanie Rademacher has designed banners made in two tones of linen for this contemporary dining area between the kitchen and garden. The colours of the linen are harmonious and calming, and the banners can be moved to create different atmospheres, depending on how you place them.

Jackye Lanham used the same semi-sheer checked fabric for curtains that are hung at the same height throughout a very large living/dining area, regardless of the shape or height of the windows or French doors, thereby creating a wonderful sense of symmetry throughout the entire space. The curtains, which have pleated headings, hang on wonderfully plain iron poles with neat brackets that keep them away from the walls and doors, and allow the doors to be opened easily.

The curved shape of bay windows often means that either you have curtains that do not close completely because of the difficulty in positioning the brackets, or you need several different curtains that draw across the bay separately. To solve this problem, designers Melanie Rademacher and Doreen Scott created a pole that had mitred and strengthened corners, and customized brackets, to allow for a bigger section of the pole to be held at the ends, preventing droop from the weight of the curtains. The bay has only one bracket at each end and a central bracket that has also been strengthened. The poles are held securely in the 20cm (8-inch) brackets, and the curtains are able to travel freely around the bay (see page 21). Another solution for a bay window, as American designer Michael Tavano suggests, is to run a curtain rod with rings across the sides of the bay, from which to hang side panels, then treat the inside of the bay with café curtains or soft Roman blinds. This solution works especially well if the bay window is not floor to ceiling.

Curtains do not have to be hung only at windows. They can also be used to cover an ugly or malformed wall, or to cover an area such as a bookshelf or closet. Curtains can also be used as room dividers in an open-plan space – for instance, to give privacy to a sleeping area in a large room.

ABOVE LEFT: A simple linen curtain is used as a room divider in this house designed by Roger Oates. Two different linens have been paired to blend with the room's furnishings, Double Stripe and Antique Linen in Teal.

LEFT: In the dramatic and elegant entrance hall of Dominique Kieffer's Paris home, banners of fabric are hung on the walls for decoration and for picture hanging. Plain dark linen curtains are hung from metal poles in the simplest but most effective way.

OPPOSITE: In an Atlanta home interior designed by Jill Vantosh, a sheer white curtain is used as a room divider, to give privacy to this master bedroom and separate it from a passage. This divider echoes the simplicity, coolness and lightness of the other curtains in the room, giving the whole area an elegant but airy feel.

ABOVE: Spectacular views of the Manhattan skyline can be seen from every window of John Barman's amazing Manhattan penthouse. This creates great drama, but also certain problems, which Barman solves or accentuates, as the case may be, on a room-by-room basis. In this spacious living area, he has used a Rogers & Goffigon fabric for neat, simple curtains, and great furniture by Fendi and Holly Hunt, to create a stunning effect with simple lines.

LEFT: Vicente Wolf has hung white linen curtains all along one wall of the dining area of an open-plan loft apartment, to soften the exposed brick wall and give the room a wonderfully soft, luminous feel. The giant opium boxes and collection of mismatching chairs around the solid dining table create an organic feel. (See also pages 44–5.)

ABOVE: Melanie Rademacher has hung these heavily lined and interlined silk curtains on a fat, industrial-looking metal pole by means of large eyelet headings. The pole has been specially designed for the shape of the bay window. The contemporary style of these almost severe-looking, beautifully tailored curtains brings the oriental figures and stunning silk cushions into relief. (See also pages 108–9.)

ABOVE RIGHT: Jackye Lanham has created a faux pelmet in duck-egg blue, to give the window height. This is a great device to add elegance to a room and make the window seem taller. The seagrass blind instantly brings a relaxed, homely feeling to the room and works well with the stone floor.

RIGHT: Hilton McConnico has chosen lilac velvet for the curtains in this Paris dining room – an unusual colour charmingly used in a very tailored way – with pale lavender silk chiffon sheers layered beneath. The red painting, one of a pair on either side of one window, is his own work, and the deep coral red, also used for a cushion, is an amazing accent in the subtle lavender-and-grey room.

Layering

THE LAYERING OF UNLINED CURTAINS IS ONE OF THE MOST SIGNIFICANT CHANGES IN CURTAIN STYLE TODAY. MANY DESIGNERS ARE USING TWO OR THREE LAYERS OF CURTAINS IN DIFFERENT WEIGHTS OR COLOURS TO GIVE MAXIMUM CHOICE AS TO HOW THEY HANG, MOVE, AND LET IN OR KEEP OUT LIGHT. IF YOU DO NOT MIND GLIMMERS OF LIGHT IN YOUR ROOMS, LAYERS WORK MUCH BETTER THAN LINED AND INTERLINED CURTAINS, WHICH APPEAR MUCH MORE SOLID. IF YOU WANT TO EXCLUDE LIGHT COMPLETELY, CONSIDER USING SHUTTERS OR BLACKOUT BLINDS TO ENABLE YOU TO ACHIEVE THE GLAMOUR OF A LESS FORMAL UNLINED LOOK.

The new softly layered curtains tend to hang on very different poles from those used for more structured curtains – simple iron ones are the poles of choice, but are not always easy to find. Unlined curtains look wonderful hung on rods from a builders' merchant. Look for simplicity and lightness when layering, as you may end up with three poles, rather than one. Pelmets are almost a thing of the past – and they are always simple and often used for a specific purpose. The poles and rings are very much on view, and there are many decorative rings available, while eyelets are also often used for light curtains. Try to choose styles that can be operated simply and do not require too many tracks and fixings, as too much machinery can spoil the effect.

ABOVE LEFT: Luigi Esposito, of the interior design and property firm Casa Forma, has used an attractive contemporary and multifunctional system of sliding panels for this top floor room in a London triplex. A sheer fabric called Kyoto by de Le Cuona in the colour Agate has been paired with a heavier fabric in worsted wool by J Robert Scott in the colour Earth. The combination is inspired – as well as screening out the light and giving easy access to the roof terrace, the panels are striking.

LEFT: Jackye Lanham's curtain maker, Willard Pitt of Atlanta, has used three colours of the same fabric to make these beautiful curtains. Creating a bespoke fabric in this way means that the stripes can be made wider or narrower, as desired. The curtains are layered over seagrass blinds, which bring great texture to the room, and the furniture and cushions blend harmoniously with this elegant window treatment (see pages 152–3).

OPPOSITE: The natural-fibre Roman blinds by Jessitt Gold, in the colour Chai with chocolate trim, echo the textures used on the walls and floor of this bedroom designed by Mary-Bryan Peyer. The blinds contrast with the light panels, made from Kravet's Sheer Cork in the colour Champagne, which are hung on unobtrusive poles by means of eyelets.

Unlined and simple does not mean easy to make. If anything, these curtains are even more difficult to achieve than complicated ones with fringes and trims, as every seam is on view. It is also essential, especially with sheer fabrics, to be very generous with the amount of fabric used to get the great free-flowing effect that epitomizes layering.

The layers can be in any order and in any weight – the finest sheers do not need to be the under-curtain, but can be used to add a dimension of glamour as well as functionality (see what Larry Laslo has achieved on pages 58–9). You can mix different weights, different colours and different textures – the choice is endless and the effects stunning. I have tried to illustrate as many of these variations as possible, so that you can show your curtain maker exactly the effect you want.

LAYERING TIPS & IDEAS

Layering that incorporates a sheer curtain or blind provides privacy without losing light, making it an ideal solution for windows that are overlooked.

When using a sheer fabric as an under-curtain, there is the option of adding a third layer – such as a blind, curtain, series of banners, screen or shutters – to cut out all the light.

There is now an enormous choice of sheer or semi-sheer fabrics and linens of all weights in different colours and designs that can be used for curtains or blinds to stunning effect.

Blinds in wonderful natural fibres, such as bamboo, hessian and banana leaf, add interest and texture to a room, especially when layered under traditional silk or linen curtains. On a practical level, they can also be used to keep out light.

OPPOSITE LEFT: The curtains in this room have been made with the attention to detail of a couture dress, in a textured silk that is folded like paper. A film of creamy gauze separates the heavy blind from the curtains, providing a further layer of interest and adding a sense of softness to this richly decorated room designed by Kelly Hoppen.

OPPOSITE RIGHT: In this room designed by Stephen Sills and James Huniford, sheer linen blinds are edged and panelled in chunky linen stripes to provide interesting texture and to create the impression of large architectural windowpanes. The blinds in fact disguise an otherwise unremarkable floor-to-ceiling window and are a perfect foil to the rich rust drapes with simple headings.

ABOVE LEFT: In the library of my London home curtain designer Doreen Scott recently replaced a rather tired-looking blind with a stunning new one made from a de Le Cuona fabric called Kyoto in the colour Topaz – it has a sort of oil-on-water moiré effect. Note the heavy border in the same fabric that gives the blind a tailored look without it being too structured. The scrim under-curtain and the khaki wool tartan, which are scooped back with a tassel, have been in the library for years, but the addition of the very stylish blind has given the whole room a new look.

ABOVE: In this bedroom designed by Kelly Hoppen, neatly tailored taupe Roman blinds slot perfectly into a tall Georgian window, its naturally elegant proportions enhanced with generous folds of white sheer silk with an eyelet heading, looped through a slim metal pole.

OPPOSITE: The bedroom in my London apartment is decorated in shades of cream and pale grey, as I find those colours very easy to live with and extremely restful. The antique gilded pelmet has been up for many years and was created by framer Antonia Scialo by joining two smaller ones together. It works well in this large room with its very high ceiling. The curtains are two layers of silk patterned with checks in cream and light buttermilk – the layers of silk are joined together loosely, rather than being lined in a traditional way. The blind is stunning – it is made from an Andrew Martin fabric called PLP01, from the Friday Collection, and has leaves captured between two layers of sheer fabric; as the light changes, the leaves become more or less visible. The daybed in front of the French doors has been re-covered in an embroidered silk, in cinnamon on cream.

ABOVE RIGHT: In this perfectly symmetrical bedroom designed by Kelly Hoppen, the horizontal detail on the voile under-curtains is echoed by the headboard and picture frame. They balance the vertical lines of the folds on the main curtains, which bring lovely texture to this calming room, in tranquil shades of pale cream and beige.

RIGHT: In a Manhattan apartment designed by Vicente Wolf, a screen has been used behind the bed to give an interesting effect to multilayering. The windows are dressed with shimmering silk French-pleated curtains and a structured sheer Roman blind – all in the cool, clean cream and butter colours in which Wolf so often works.

Today's sheers are exciting, new and very versatile. They are no longer just fine white linen, simple muslin or mosquito netting, used in a secondary role under the main curtain or to hide an ugly view.

SHEERS

Sheers now come in many fabrics; they can be in any colour, plain, patterned, embroidered or appliquéd – and they can be used in endless creative ways to make a style statement in their own right.

plain & simple

Airy Billowing Diaphanous Thin Transparent Hazy Muslin Fine Linen Organdie Summer Breeze Sea Mist Zephyr Cloud April Showers Buttermilk Taupe Pearl Mushroom Stone Vanilla Antique White Ivory Ice Cube Chalk Egg White

Chic and classic, understated sheers in various textures and weights are staple curtain fabrics. Versatile in their use – either layered or on their own – they can be billowy or tailored, glamorous or simple. In today's interiors we require light, privacy and flexibility. Sheer fabrics, cleverly designed and used, fulfil all of these needs.

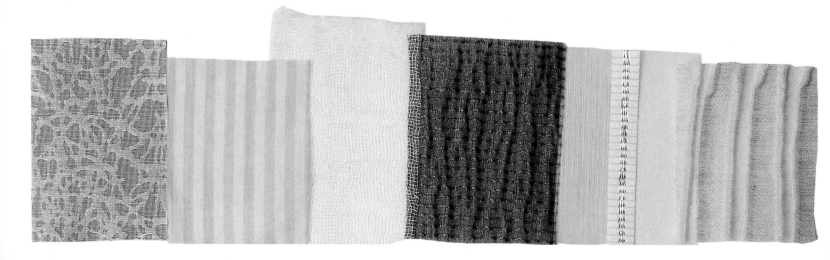

THIS PAGE AND OPPOSITE: A fabric called Gloss, a linen and polyester blend by Pollack, was used for the curtains in the informal dining area of this Atlanta home designed by Tim Hobby. The fabric, which has a metallic thread, looks and feels like silk but, being a synthetic, is more resilient against the strong Georgia sunlight. The light, slightly glossy fabric is airy and cool, and the perfect foil for the custom bronze and walnut table by Blackman Cruz and the light fixture by Holly Hunt. The curtain heading is simple and tailored, letting the fabric fall in soft, even folds. The ceiling cornice above the bay window conceals the mechanism for the motorized curtains, which are worked by remote control from a switch on the wall. Motorized curtains can offer a practical solution when curtains are behind furniture and hard to reach, but this approach needs to be decided on as early as possible in the design process, so that the workings and track can be concealed dicreetly within the design. Seagrass blinds are an attractive addition to the French doors leading out into the garden.

the changing face of sheers

Sheer fabrics first made their mark in the world of interior design in the form of plain linen, cotton, voile or muslin – in any and all shades of white – made up into very simple light, billowy curtains to use in beach or country cottages, either floating freely or held with a tieback. Gradually came the introduction of sheer under-curtains layered beneath the main curtains, then came the layers of sheer curtains in different weights, on separate rails so that they could be drawn singly or together. Sheers are now indisputably key contenders in the wardrobe of curtain fabrics and styles.

And with curtain designers increasingly using unlined fabrics, the need for sheers as under-curtains has increased, and new ways of expressing this layered look are much in evidence.

Sheers are not always floaty and feminine; they can and often are chic and urban. Designer Vicente Wolf is a past master in using wonderful semi-sheer fabrics for Roman blinds in urban settings. Neat and elegant, they are the perfect backdrop for the rooms he designs. Sheer panels also work well in urban surroundings – fixed top and bottom, almost like floating screens, or fixed only at the top so that they can be moved along rails for different effects.

THIS PAGE: In the fabulous and fascinating Paris apartment of Dominique Kieffer, each room is a treat, with special fabrics and curtain styles. In this very glamorous – not to mention well-organized – dressing room, the curtain drops elegantly on rings from the most simple pole, and hangs in gentle folds to the floor. The soft, cool white 100 per cent linen sheer, called Pastel à Indio, is from Kieffer's own range of stunning fabrics.

OPPOSITE LEFT: This simple-to-make heading seen on a sheer curtain at Cape Grace hotel is a perfect solution when the sheers are beneath the main drapes, as they so often are. The voile, muslin or organza – in this case, polyester voile – is gathered onto a Rufflette pencil-pleat tape, giving the effect of a laboriously constructed smocked heading and achieving fullness with little effort. The curtain then hooks onto rings on a pole – just make sure that you use enough hooks, so that it does not dip.

OPPOSITE TOP RIGHT: A sheer voile curtain by Jill Vantosh drops casually from plain rings and a pole, and drapes in informal folds. This is a very easy way to make a light curtain and can hit all the right notes in a casual way. I love the uncluttered look of iron poles and rings.

OPPOSITE BOTTOM RIGHT: A smocked heading is a much more complicated and professional curtain heading than those formed by using a standard heading tape, but it is very effective when used in a feminine setting, as it is here in a bedroom designed by Jackye Lanham (see also pages 170–71). The pretty effect is accentuated by the velvet ribbons that tie the curtain onto the iron pole. The juxtaposition of the utilitarian iron pole and the ultra-feminine curtain works perfectly.

HEADINGS FOR SHEER CURTAINS TOP TIPS

Sheer curtains need to be full – if you use too little fabric, they will look mean and skimpy. To achieve the desired fullness, you need a generous width of fabric.

Many curtain makers use a gathered or very finely pleated heading – resulting in an almost smocked effect – in order to get the fabric to fall in neat, elegant and manageable folds.

In many cases, this can be effectively achieved by using a specialized curtain heading tape, such as a Rufflette pencil-pleat or smocked-pleat tape, which can be sewn onto the back of the sheer curtain and used to gather the fabric.

This is not to say that you cannot use the more traditional pinch-pleated – or French-pleated – and goblet-pleated headings for sheer curtains, but in my opinion a more gathered or finely pleated heading will give a better, if less tailored, effect.

Whatever type of heading you choose, in terms of hardware to complement your sheer curtains, it is a definite fact that iron is in. In addition to simple rings, unusual decorative hooks made of iron are beginning to emerge and these add great interest to the heading of a curtain. Interesting iron hardware can also be most attractive when used between curtains on the wall at the heading level. (See also pages 180–187.)

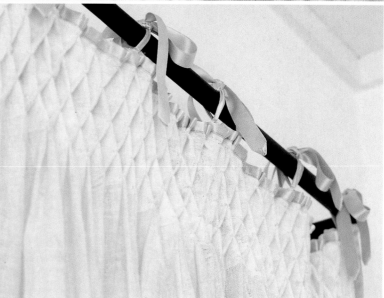

THIS PAGE: The beautiful and elegant sheer white curtains used by Jill Vantosh in this Atlanta drawing room are a triumph of design – the contrast against the dark wood floor adds great depth to the room. The sheer fabric is from Coraggio Textiles and is bordered along the bottom edge with a broad band of Libas silk, to add some weight.

OPPOSITE: The dining room of the same house is a much darker, moodier room. It has the same dark floor, but also dark furniture, and it faces another direction. Vantosh has used simple sheer blinds on the windows of the bay, leaving the decorative top panels free – this is an important touch, as they are a feature of the room. The curtain at the French door has been looped up with cord to make access easy. The same Coraggio fabric has been used, but this time it has been trimmed down the side with a ribbon of Libas silk in dark green, to provide definition. The house is full of well-chosen details such as great chandeliers and art.

BED HANGINGS JACKYE LANHAM

Traditionally, bed hangings were used to keep out the cold and to discourage animals and bugs, so they should draw all the way around the bed, enclosing it entirely.

Create a 'room' for the bed, by suspending iron rods from the ceiling that are wider and longer than the bed. The curtained space can contain a bedside table, lamp and chest at the foot of the bed. This is cosy and practical, especially in a shared room.

A cold climate dictates heavy, lush interlined bed curtains, while a warm climate calls for gauzy, cool fabrics such as mosquito netting, or any of the lovely new sheers.

Get creative – use a plain fabric on the outside of the curtain and a patterned one on the inside, or make a handkerchief valance instead of a traditional gathered or pleated heading.

For a chic modern look, use thin iron rods around the bed; hang the curtains from small iron rings, or tie them onto the bed frame with spaghetti ties or long flat ties – nothing heavy or cumbersome. The lightest sheers can be hung from a fine rod, simply threaded through a simple heading.

ABOVE AND OPPOSITE: The simplicity of these lightly embroidered off-white muslin bed curtains is perfect for a seaside home, as they look cool and welcoming, as well as keeping the mosquitoes out. The curtains, which have virtually no hem and simple headings with ties, hang from slim iron poles around a pair of beds in a guest room designed by Jackye Lanham. The blue-and-white rug and dark shutters at the windows are a great contrast to the softness of the drapes. The same shade of blue is used on the bed base and the lovely French pillowcases.

LEFT: Lanham has given the muslin sheers on this traditional wooden bedstead a more formal treatment. The gathered curtains are hung on a narrow-gauge track and have a deep hem that adds weight to the way the fabric falls. The embroidery is a lovely couture touch. The window drapes are much heavier and are hung on iron rods (see also pages 78–9).

OPPOSITE: A charming checked semi-sheer fabric has been masterfully used by Jackye Lanham in the dining room of a comfortable but very elegant seaside home on Sea Island, Georgia. Where the curtains are drawn, light streams through in a diffuse manner, giving the room a golden glow. This soft, filmy sheer is an Arabel fabric. (See also pages 14–15.)

THIS PAGE: In a Manhattan apartment, Vicente Wolf has used a full sheer linen curtain to create a room divider between a library that leads off a living area and a passage to the bedrooms. The library is separated from the passage by a double-sided transparent bookcase containing not only books, but also *objets trouvés*. The linen curtain covers the passage side of the bookcase and also forms a curtained 'wall' between the library and the living area, making a perfect occasional guest room. This innovative use of fabric leaves the area light and airy, with or without the division. (See also pages 44–5.)

OPPOSITE: Jackye Lanham has created a delightful overhanging valance with this deceptively simple sheer curtain in a North Florida home. The curtains hang from simple iron hooks on a fabulous iron pole, creating the perfect look for a beach house. The cotton bobble fringe on the edge of the valance adds definition and charm.

RIGHT: In this Manhattan apartment interior designed by Vicente Wolf, the entrance from the hall to the dining room is a multifunctional screen door with fabric panels, which can be opened in several ways. The fabric adds another layer to both the hall and the dining room, giving a much more interesting look and feel than an ordinary solid wall or doors would give, and creating a softer, more elegant space.

BELOW: In my kitchen at home, I have enough space to store everything, prepare and cook food, and have as many as ten to dine with me. One wall is all windows, as in a previous lifetime the kitchen was several rooms. Curtain designer Doreen Scott made me soft blinds from a sort of 'dishcloth' fabric, with a banner of suede down the middle. They allow all the light in during the day, and views onto the trees outside, but maintain our privacy when we are eating at night.

This wonderful New York apartment – a former industrial space, with its superb girders and beams still in place – has been transformed into a comfortable, liveable home by interior designer Vicente Wolf. With the innovative and versatile use of his signature white linen fabrics in different weights, he has made this large, open space multifunctional, without being rigid or static.

Wolf's work is all about finding elegant, easy living solutions for specific people, rather than simply following a design philosophy. Here, using different weights of sheer and semi-sheer linen fabric, he has created a tranquil haven for his clients in the midst of this frenetic, noisy city.

The windows – the traditional place for curtains – have simple folded Roman blinds that suit the architectural strength of this building and the proportions of the room. The series of blinds aligns perfectly across the entire window section, engendering a great feeling of calm.

They allow in light, but still provide the level of privacy needed.

Wolf has completely covered one wall of the living area with a sweep of lightweight, flowing linen, which is slightly coarser but the same colour as the blinds. The wall hanging uses a generous amount of fabric – the key to ensuring that sheer linen curtains look luxurious –

and the heading is a neat, unfussy pleat on a basic track. Both simple and unexpected, the wall-covering curtain adds a sense of softness and comfort to the room.

Another sheer linen fabric has been used along both sides of the bookcase that borders the passage to the bedroom, and between the guest room/library and the main living area. These curtains are hung in such a way as to align with the track lights and beams in this part of the space. The room-dividing curtain is a great design solution. When this curtain is open, the entire space is very large, with dining, seating and reading areas all leading into one another. Covering just one side of the bookcase makes a passage to the bedroom. Covering both sides and the side facing the living area forms a private room for a guest, without losing light or the sense of space.

Wolf's clever use of fabric softens the open-plan space and gives it flexibility. By keeping to the same colour and type of fabric throughout, he ensures that the space's unity and elegance are not compromised.

COLOURED SHEERS TOP TIPS

Coloured sheers are a new and exciting addition to the ever-growing variety of sheers that the twenty-first century seems to have produced. Such companies as de Le Cuona, Dominique Kieffer and Kravet have always had wonderful sheer fabrics in cotton, linen and organza, but the colour spectrum, although filled with variations, was always within the white, cream and ecru range. Now one can find an amazing selection of coloured sheers, both decorative and plain.

While coloured sheers can create a fabulous effect, I suggest that they are used with caution. Any amateur can choose a good neutral tone and make a successful window of sheers, both as main drapes and as under-curtains. When it comes to the colours, however, the effect can go horribly wrong unless they are chosen with great care.

Coloured sheers come into their own when the main curtain is a deep colour and the contrast of a white or cream sheer underneath it would be too extreme and jarring; in this instance, a sheer curtain in a lighter shade of the main fabric would work well, producing a subtle, more cohesive effect.

ABOVE AND LEFT: Instead of cream or white sheers, Hilton McConnico often uses a plain coloured sheer in a shade that matches the main drapes, so as to totally unify the colour of the window. Sheers in the orange, red and pink colour spectrum will warm up the light, while greens and blues tend to give a cooler feel.

OPPOSITE: Here McConnico has used a burnt orange/red sheer fabric for the under-curtain in this all-orange bedroom, to add to the sense of colour and warmth. The burnt orange of the sheers is a perfect foil for the stripe on the chair.

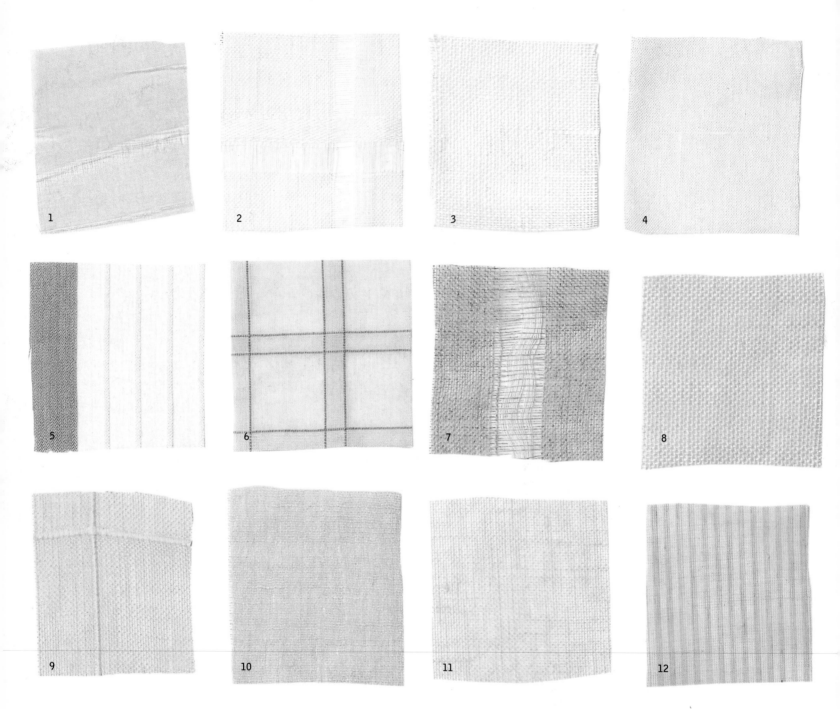

SWATCHES

ABOVE: In addition to plain 100 per cent linen sheers in different weights and shades, from fine and coarse white (4 and 3), to fine and coarse beige (10 and 8), to fine pale green (11), other finishes and weaves that manufacturers have created add an interesting dimension to the sheer effect, such as the sheers with open pulled-thread stripes and checks (2 and 7) and raised embroidered checks, shown here in a soft yellow (9). Simple striped and checked cotton sheers (6 and 12) are available in many subtle shades that work well under toning plain curtains, while other synthetic sheers with colourful stripes (5) and gold threads running through it (1) can be used to make a glamorous statement.

OPPOSITE BACKGROUND: Pale cream medium-weave linen is a sheer that works in just about any context for curtains and blinds alike.

OPPOSITE TOP LEFT: Edging a blind with the same fabric in a contrasting colour is the ideal way to create interest – you can edge all the way around, or just both sides or the base. Using a dark colour along the edge, such as this soft coffee-coloured linen on the same buttermilk linen, is also practical, as that is the area most likely to be touched.

OPPOSITE BOTTOM LEFT: Patterned sheers can also be edged with plain fabric, such as this narrow striped cotton voile, which has been gathered and edged with matching plain green linen. This type of border could be used on the heading of a curtain to conceal the gathered edge and track.

OPPOSITE RIGHT: A simple gathered heading is perfect for attaching a curtain to a tension-wire-and-hooks system. This is ideal for a light sheer, such as this peach linen with embroidered self-stripe.

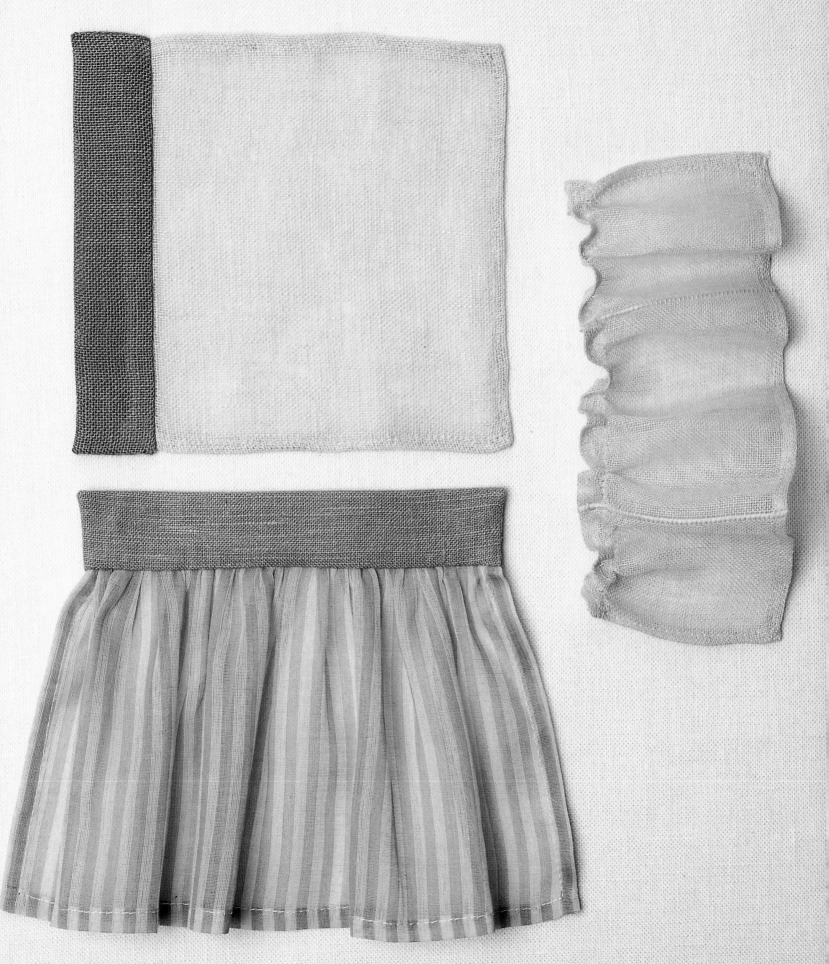

decorative

Light and Breezy Gauzy Filmy Opaque See-through Gossamer Oyster Shadows Waterfall White-Water Rapids Smoke Moonshine Appliqué Embroidery Tone on Tone Self-Stripe Lace Moire Paisley Beading Stitching

In many ways, the explosion of new designs in sheer fabrics has inspired new and innovative ways of dressing windows, in addition to the tried and tested. The range of decorative sheers is so diverse and wondrous, and the fabrics are so versatile, that making a choice can be bewildering. These fabrics are no afterthought, but true style statements.

new innovations

New York-based designer Larry Laslo's philosophy is that everything that meets the eye should be beautiful, and that an interior space should be punctuated with colour, motifs and exquisite detail to make it sing. Having surveyed the variety of sheer fabrics on the market, he realized that there were very few dark or intensely coloured sheers, if any at all. There were also very few designs with large repeats, so he set out to fill the void when he created his phenomenal collection of decorative sheers for Robert Allen. These included stunning tone-on-tone fabrics, where ribbons of frayed silk were appliquéd onto a fine sheer base fabric in various designs from stripes to swirls. The inspiration for the glamorous fabric used for the bed curtains in his apartment (see opposite) was his vision of a Valentino gown paired with a cashmere sweater.

OPPOSITE AND BELOW: For the curtains on this iron bed, Larry Laslo chose one of my favourites from his new range of sheers for Robert Allen, Freshness in the colour Earth. Slices of frayed fabric have been appliquéd onto the background sheer to form regular stripes – the chance that the edges may continue to fray is only a possible plus. The lightness of this sheer gives the room an ethereal feel, and light streaming through the windows creates an ever-changing effect. The softness and glamour of the bed curtains are a foil for the elegant Roman blinds in a striped fabric called Generous in the colour Rosewood, and silk cushions in jewel colours.

DECORATIVE SHEERS TOP TIPS

One of designer Larry Laslo's favourite devices is to hang two different sheers on a double rod, so that they can be drawn separately to give a two-tone effect. This technique can also be used to allow less or more light into a room.

Another new effect used by Laslo turns traditional layering on its head – layering a sheer curtain over instead of under one of taffeta or velvet, or another plain or patterned fabric, to create a glamorous see-through couture look (see pages 58–9).

Piping the edges of plain or decorative pure white, off-white, ecru and other neutral-toned sheer curtains or blinds with a strong colour can be very effective, giving a sense of form, shape and definition. This can be used on either the blind or the curtain, or on both together for maximum impact.

Embroidery – in contrasting colour, or tone on tone – is another striking way to dress up an otherwise simple sheer curtain or blind. Butterflies, bees and other insects, bows, flowers and geometric patterns are perennially popular, while more unusual designs include a series of Roman numerals.

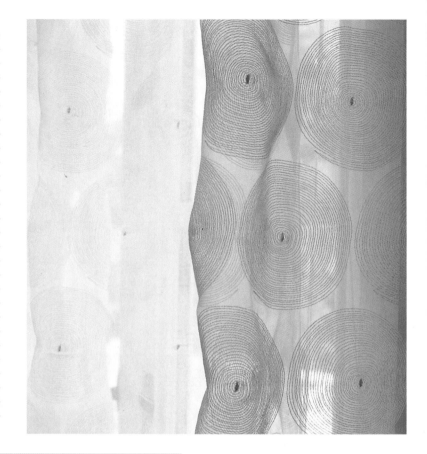

ABOVE: Embroidered sheers create a pretty, feminine effect and are available in many designs, from florals and botanicals to geometrics, such as this Kravet fabric, Sheer with Embroidery Circles in the colour Snow.

LEFT: Dominique Kieffer has used a stunning sheer white linen with a strong pattern 'etched' into it called Jasmin de Nuit in the colour Blanc for the under-curtains in her Paris apartment. They hang with the main curtain on an unobtrusive double iron track from simple rings – the whole structure seems to float.

OPPOSITE: This bathroom at Bishopsgrace guesthouse in Cape Town was designed by Kathi Weixelbaumer. The grey and white toile curtains with heavy cotton fringe match ones in the adjoining bedroom, but here she has used a sheer voile café curtain embroidered with Roman numerals by a local embroiderer, giving maximum light and privacy.

statement sheers Fabric designers and manufacturers such as Robert Allen and Kravet have recently excelled at bringing a steady stream of beautiful decorative sheers into their ranges – not only in neutral shades of white, cream and taupe, but also in rich colours such as plum and moss green. Many of these new sheers feature wonderful patterns that create light and shadow in glamorous and interesting ways, or embroidery that is either subtle and discreet or bold and abundant. These exciting fabrics cry out to be more than supplementary curtains, but rather to be used in their own right to dramatically change the look of a room. Appliquéd, lace or heavily embroidered sheers add a different dimension of changing light patterns to a room, while the more subtly patterned and embellished examples bring a feminine, romantic touch.

ABOVE LEFT: All the bedrooms in a Sea Island house designed by Mary-Bryan Peyer have sheers and blinds at their windows, giving each room a look of freshness and ease. This room is a symphony of blues, ecrus and whites. The decorative sheers hanging from an iron pole, with simple but elegant headings, are a fabric called Cross Stitch Vine in Ecru by Kravet, and the Roman blinds beneath are made up in Cooper House Ikat by Greeff Fabrics, in Blue. The same sheers hang from the iron bedstead (not seen), while the ikat is used again for upholstery, echoing the window treatment and giving the room uniformity.

ABOVE: Here the Roman blinds are white with black trim, under a Kravet fabric called Sheer with Embroidery Circles in the colour Snow. The natural tones of the upholstered bed and the pistachio colours of the throws on the white quilt complete this crisp-looking room.

OPPOSITE: In another bedroom a natural-fibre blind is hung under dramatic decorative sheers. These are slotted through a metal pole with metal eyelets, giving the room a contemporary look. The cinnamon and cream colour scheme accented with the striped bedlinen is truly chic.

CASE STUDY GLAMOUR & INNOVATION

Designer Larry Laslo rose to the challenge when a somewhat soulless 1950s apartment building was chosen for the annual Kips Bay Decorator Show House, instead of the usual town house location. Laslo, one of 22 designers given rooms there to decorate for the show, took one look at the space, with its low ceilings and rather unattractive windows, and decided it was Hollywood come to Manhattan. The black-and-white movies of the postwar period, the music of Cole Porter and the ritziness of Palm Springs were his inspirations. The resulting apartment is so stunning and redolent of the great era of glamour that the initial design shortcomings of the rooms become insignificant.

In the spacious living room, with its large window and sliding doors out onto the terrace, Laslo has done something unusual – to great dramatic effect – in reversing the role of the sheer fabric in the curtain treatment. Usually, the sheer is the fabric that is used under the main curtain fabric, creating the less important layer in terms of style and aesthetics. In this room, Laslo has teamed two of his stunning new fabrics for Robert Allen in a very theatrical way. The heavier fabric, a moss-green pure silk taffeta, is the under-curtain, and the kiwi-green Many Facets sheer is the over-curtain. Paired together, the two fabrics create a magnificent wall of colour and pattern, but when the taffeta is drawn back underneath and the sheer covers the window on its own, a totally different look takes over the room. A triumph of innovation, this unconventional use of fabric is a fascinating design solution, as it keeps one's eye away from the ceiling heights and lack of architectural features, and all the focus on the drama of the fabric used for the curtains.

Laslo has injected more colour and excitement with his great choice of photographic artwork, zebra-print rug, Venetian plaster and silver. Together with the organic furniture shapes, these accents bring pure 1950s Bel Air to Manhattan.

By adding both pattern and colour to his remarkable new collection of sheer fabrics, Laslo has almost reinvented the look of sheers and made them a major decorative fabric choice, rather than a simple, practical under-curtain or layer of light fabric. A real style statement in their own right, sheers can now spell out glamour, either used on their own or, as here, when teamed with a heavier fabric.

SHEER BLINDS TOP TIPS

Interior designers have used sheer fabrics for blinds for some time, particularly in urban areas where there is a need for privacy while maximizing natural light in the interior. Vicente Wolf, for example, has always used wonderful sheer linen blinds in one form or another, and always at exactly the same level if they run along a stretch of glazing, offering elegance, privacy and some relief from direct sunlight.

Both elegant and practical, sheer blinds are a staple of many of today's interiors. They can be made from fine cotton or linen, muslin, synthetic fibres and fabrics made from plants such as banana skin. They can range from the starkly simple to the decorative and elaborate, and from roller to Roman. Think carefully about what look you would like your blind to bring to your room, and decide on the style and fabric accordingly.

An alternative to a roller or Roman blind is a sliding panel blind, which is pulled across the window rather than up and down, and can be layered behind dress curtains. The panels can be alternating colours – say, ivory and cinnamon – or a single colour. Remember, a dark colour will block out more light.

OPPOSITE: Larry Laslo has used one of his own designs for Robert Allen, Many Facets in the colour Kiwi, for this softly folded Roman blind. It is a perfect decorative sheer with a great all-over pattern, which creates interest and great sophistication without blocking out any of the light.

ABOVE: This simple semi-sheer blind features the outline of a blue flower in the centre, giving an arresting and attractive effect, while blocking out virtually no light. The window is one of a series in the long passage of the Haymarket Hotel in London, designed by Kit Kemp. The fabric was specially printed to tie in with the wallpaper, and the combination creates interest in this potentially dreary area.

LEFT: Jackye Lanham has used a Cowtan & Tout die-cut fabric lined with a soft blue chintz for a Roman blind in her kitchen, giving a very interesting and unusual look to this window.

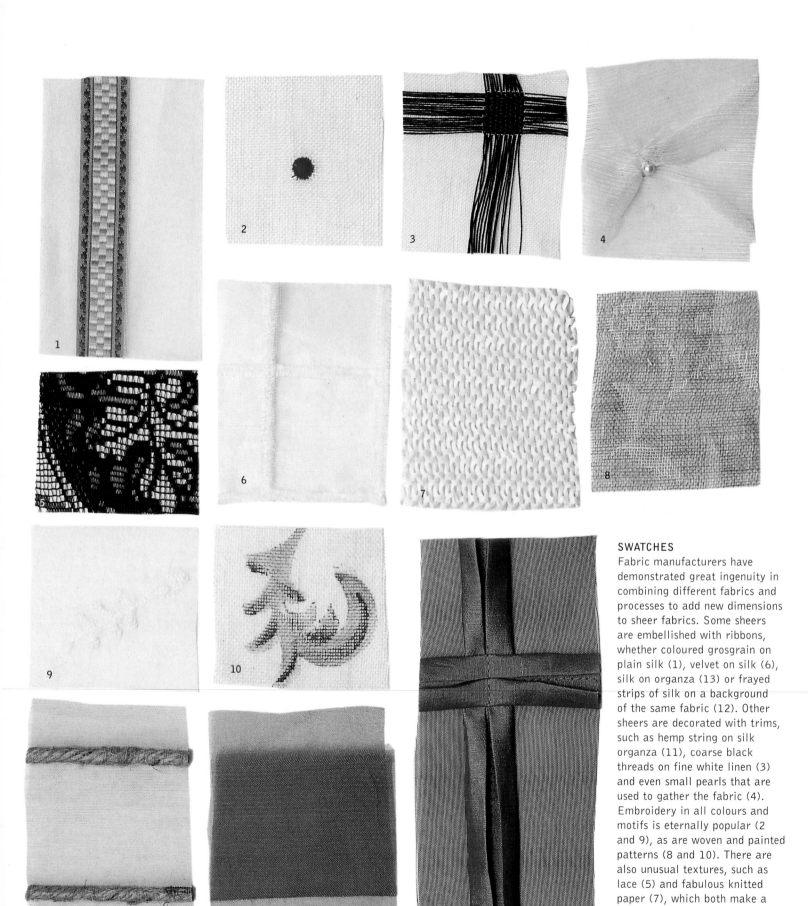

SWATCHES

Fabric manufacturers have demonstrated great ingenuity in combining different fabrics and processes to add new dimensions to sheer fabrics. Some sheers are embellished with ribbons, whether coloured grosgrain on plain silk (1), velvet on silk (6), silk on organza (13) or frayed strips of silk on a background of the same fabric (12). Other sheers are decorated with trims, such as hemp string on silk organza (11), coarse black threads on fine white linen (3) and even small pearls that are used to gather the fabric (4). Embroidery in all colours and motifs is eternally popular (2 and 9), as are woven and painted patterns (8 and 10). There are also unusual textures, such as lace (5) and fabulous knitted paper (7), which both make a great decorative statement.

BACKGROUND: Indian linen with gold embroidered dots adds a touch of exotic glamour.

BELOW LEFT: The silk dupion used for the edging is similar in tone to the main fabric – a wonderfully glamorous silk with embroidery in a squiggle pattern. This demonstrates how different textures in the same colour can be introduced on one curtain or blind.

BELOW RIGHT: Timberland in Mica, by Larry Laslo for Robert Allen, has been edged in dark grey ribbon. This is a similar effect to that in Laslo's dining room (see page 51), where the same fabric has been edged in a border the same colour as the main fabric.

BOTTOM: Dominique Kieffer's Jasmin de Nuit is gathered simply, demonstrating how one of my favourite sheers would look gathered onto tension wire.

Natural fabrics have never been more in demand. With the increasing awareness of ecological issues, fabrics with a 'from the earth' feeling have become key players in the world of design.

NATURALS

Linens and cottons abound, and the choice is wondrous – from the roughest hand-woven naturals, to fine textiles in sophisticated tones. A new and exciting advance is the wider availability of organic fabrics.

cottons & linens

Natural Irish Linen Calico Fine Cotton Lawn Hopsack Flax Hemp Canvas Sackcloth Pure Organic Scrim Seersucker Cambric Holland Jute Woven Twine String Oatmeal Biscuit Barley Porridge Slubby Wheat Crumpled Stonewashed

The reassuring textures of natural linen and cotton fabrics are guaranteed to bring a relaxed, comfortable feel to a home. These fabrics are the 'little black dresses' of curtains – they go with everything and complement most interior settings and decorating styles, from loft apartments to period homes, from country cottages to beach houses.

sophisticated elegance

Synonymous with the fashionably crumpled summer clothes worn on the Italian Riviera, linen cannot be beaten for understated chic. A natural fibre made from flax, linen is perfect for hot weather, as it lets the skin breathe – and it is not just confined to the wardrobe. Linen sheets are luxury to sleep on and, thanks to designers such as Bernie de Le Cuona and John England, linen fabrics of all weights and textures are perennially popular choices for curtains, blinds and other furnishings. The various weaves and finishes can be used to achieve many looks, from simple and rustic, to smart and sophisticated. There is something about the weave that makes linen instantly recognizable as a material that is natural and pure, and this is a large part of its appeal in a predominantly synthetic world.

OPPOSITE: The white curtains add to the elegant contemporary feel of this conservatory-like living area designed by Andrzej Zarzycki. They have been slotted, with nickel rings, over a nickel-plated pole – a modern way to give a home a new look.

ABOVE: In this Paris bedroom, simple but elegant free-flowing cream curtains are made in Lainage by Dominique Kieffer and lined with Euco Blanc made of organic cotton – something Kieffer is adding to her range more and more. The sheers are Jasmin de Nuit in Blanc.

design inspiration A well-designed room offers an immediate sensation of comfort that encourages relaxation and puts people at ease. This is partly achieved when a look seems to have come together effortlessly, as if it has evolved naturally, rather than having been 'designed'.

I always advise people to find a favourite object, painting or piece of china, and use that as their starting point for a scheme – it makes the whole process easier. Interior designer Jackye Lanham does this with the flair of a master, often taking inspiration for her colour palettes from treasured objects or collections of ceramics, shells and sea glass. In her own home, she creates wonderful groups of objects that add layer upon layer to her living and dining room, which she has decorated in a palette of soft teal blue, darker sea blue, ivory and shell colours, for an eclectic yet harmonious whole. The curtains she chose to complement this scheme are made from 100 per cent cotton seersucker with overscaled puckering in ivory/cream. The perfect choice for a relaxed 'beach home' look, they hang from blacksmith-made iron curtain rods by means of spaghetti ties.

LEFT: The shelves over the seating unit in this 'inspiration corner' display all the items that inspired Jackye Lanham in her creation of this perfect living room in her beach house in North Florida. Having an object, a colour or a combination of both as a starting point makes it much easier to achieve the colour choices and the intended feel of a room.

ABOVE: In the same delightful room overlooking the Atlantic Ocean and white sandy beaches, the cotton seersucker fabric with overscaled puckering was an inspired choice for the curtains. It gives the room an airy, summery feel, especially hanging as it does from the blacksmith-made iron curtain rods by means of long spaghetti ties.

OPPOSITE: The wall of curtains acts as a foil for the stone floor and provides a neutral backdrop for the pale blue cushions and throws, shell pictures and subtle colours that together create the perfect ambiance.

BUTTONS TOP TIPS

Buttons have long been used as a decorative element on cushions, but now they are also very much in vogue as an adornment on curtains, adding texture, colour and detail.

An eclectic collection of vintage buttons could be used for an informal feel, while matching buttons create a smarter, more uniform look. Mother-of-pearl buttons are very effective on most weights, types and colours of fabric, as they are neutral in tone, catch the light and give a unique textural interest.

Buttons can be used as a decorative feature on curtains in several ways: to delineate the seam between two different fabrics; to anchor pleats on the curtain heading; or simply as a decorative trimming along the hem or border.

OPPOSITE AND ABOVE: On simple semi-sheer curtains at a beach house in Florida, Jackye Lanham has used rows of buttons – dark tortoiseshell on white as an interesting contrast – to form and define the pleat and add to the interesting effect of the basic iron pole and hooks. This is a laid-back curtain style that can be adapted in many ways and used on different plain fabrics for a really effective designer look.

LEFT: Interior designer Kit Kemp has used mother-of-pearl buttons and two different but matching linen fabrics to make a simple curtain look innovative and amazingly stylish. The combination of the heavy, plain blue stonewashed linen and the narrow stripe in cream and beige is effective, but, once the mother-of-pearl buttons are added, sewn neatly and evenly onto a plain cream band between the two fabrics, the curtain suddenly becomes 'couture'. Buttons have been used for some time to decorate cushions, and now we see this great look being transferred to curtains in a very effective way.

CASE STUDY ELEGANT LAYERING

Interior designer Mimmi O'Connell has always had a style totally her own, which has evolved and matured over time and is always fresh and cutting-edge in the best possible way. Inherently liveable, her work fits unerringly into the way one wants to live today.

Her London home is refined and simple, with wonderful fabrics perfectly made up into curtains and soft furnishings, and lots of unique styling ideas. These clever touches, together with all of the things she loves – Chinese furniture and objects, vintage textiles, painted oak floors, and rooms devoid of art on the walls but with dramatic pieces such as an oversized Japanese screen – combine to create comfort and a feeling of easy living.

The living room is a symphony of soft, elegant fabrics, in shades of white, cream, taupe and brown. The daybeds are upholstered in striped cotton by Pierre Frey, and the sofa has a tufted, buttoned beige mattress

that is so chic against the heavy off-white linen. The dark wood furniture against the cream floor engenders a sense of tranquillity and excitement coexisting side by side, making a room that is perfect for all occasions.

O'Connell's use of fabrics in this room is seemingly simple, but the textures, tones and weights have been perfectly chosen to blend with each other. Like me, she prefers the way curtain fabric hangs when it is unlined, and prefers layers rather than linings. Two separate curtains hang at each of the three floor-to-ceiling windows, and they can be drawn in several ways for different effects – we loved them most when the top layer was pulled halfway back, creating the illusion of one curtain with a wide vertical border. The curtains hang from simple dark waxed steel poles, slotted through discreet eyelets (see page 181). Each curtain, in different weights of Irish linen from John England, has an oversized border – a lovely new touch in modern window treatments – in oyster and cream, and oyster with dark buff. Behind the two layers of curtains are antique Japanese sudari blinds. The clever window treatment makes this calm room feel cosy in winter and airy in summer.

LEFT: African Sketchbook, a small eco-friendly company in Cape Town that employs men and women from the surrounding townships to hand-paint cotton, linen, velvet and silk for curtains, was given a challenge – the client wanted curtains to match the grey marble in this stunningly original bathroom at Cape Grace hotel. The locally milled, off-white, 100 per cent cotton hopsack was painstakingly painted the exact colour of the marble, using large brushes to retain the hand-painted effect. Finally, the calligraphy was silkscreened on drape by drape and always in pairs to ensure perfect balance. The simple fall-forward style was used on a fully gathered curtain. The antique butter churn used as a laundry basket is an inspired touch.

OPPOSITE: The living room of this charming apartment in Paris designed by Hilton McConnico is both tailored and softly elegant, with three soft colours – delicate shades of lime, lavender and grey – blending together to create a subtle look. The curtains with their simple pleats and sheers form the perfect backdrop to the exquisite settee.

TUFTED 'QUILT' CURTAINS & BLINDS

These wonderful thick tufted curtains and blind were made for interior designer Jackye Lanham by Willard Pitt Curtain Makers of Atlanta, Georgia. Triple cotton wadding is the foundation, making a curtain that is neither too thin nor too fat, but rather the lovely weight of an old quilt – something soft and cuddly that exudes a sense of warmth and comfort.

One can, of course, vary the fabrics that one uses to cover the wadding, but Lanham suggests that two different fabrics are always used to create a contrast border – for example, two different textures and colours of linen or wool, or even a mixture of wool and silk. In the master bedroom of her beach house (below and opposite), she used two weights of Irish linen. The curtain is hung on a simple iron pole for a casual, breezy look, using small-scale iron rings sewn onto the top edge – such a clever touch for a heading.

To form the tufts that create the cosy eiderdown effect, Lanham says that they always pull a colour-related string through the centre panel at regular intervals, to give the fabrics stability and added detail.

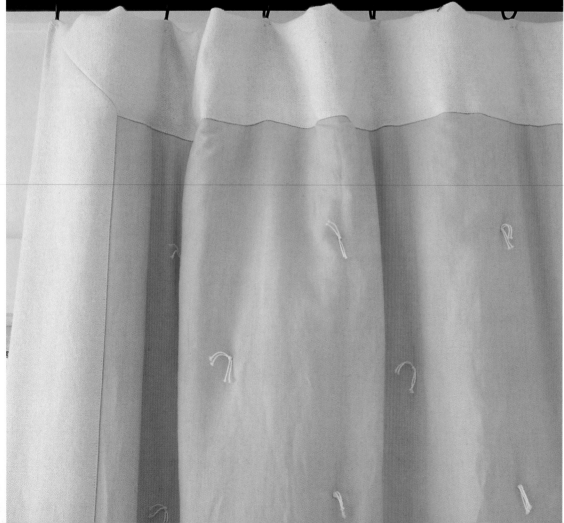

ABOVE: In a beach house near Jacksonville, Florida, Jackye Lanham has used a pale blue Travers fabric, together with very heavy lining and interlining, to create the effect of an almost quilted fabric. The wide cream border gives a custom-designed touch to the simple blind. The effect is more bedcover than blind, and this brings a real comfort factor to the room.

LEFT AND OPPOSITE: In the master bedroom of her beach house, Jackye Lanham has used a Cowtan & Tout fabric for the curtains. The buttercup-coloured fabric has been heavily lined and interlined – a construction achieved with wadding, rather like a comforter or old-fashioned eiderdown. It is almost as if Lanham had found a pair of vintage quilts and converted them into curtains to make her bedroom warm and cosy. Once again, the wide borders give the curtains an appealing customized feel.

colour & texture
Linen used to be available in only the very natural colours – cream, ivory and pale beige – but now the choice is endless, from subtle earthy taupes and soft greens and blues, through the rich shades of spices, to deep chocolate and navy. Vicente Wolf's words, 'If the colour appears in nature, it is going to be a good colour,' provide an apt motto for this type of fabric – the colours of food, in particular, are perfect.

Indeed, the different weights, textures and weaves also seem to be endless, with fabrics being manufactured not only in Belgium, Italy and Ireland, but all over the Far East as well. Linens range from light and sheer, to very heavy and textured. Texture is important, and the rough weave of linen brings a down-to-earth individuality to a room and contrasts well with the smooth surfaces of walls and floors.

Layers of linen curtains in different weights or shades are stunning and always look effortlessly chic. A word of warning: as is the case with so many really simple ideas, it is more complex to achieve this look successfully than it at first appears. While pelmets and valances could hide many ugly secrets, free-hanging linen curtains on uncomplicated iron poles hide nothing – it is all on view, and every stitch has to be perfect, every pleat evenly placed.

OPPOSITE AND RIGHT: In this corner of her living room in Paris, Dominique Kieffer has used, once again, two almost industrial rods from which to hang her linen curtains and Jasmin de Nuit sheers by means of tiny rings. This simple method truly lets the fabrics do the talking. The lining, called Moustique – and it is really another layer of fabric, rather than a lining – can be clearly seen, making an original statement. Using another fabric in this way, instead of a traditional lining, serves as a contrast, a weight difference and an enhancer to the main curtain fabric, called Tozan, in the colour Fuchsia.

'To complement the understated elegance of fabrics such as cotton and linen, furnishings and styling should be all about subtraction not addition, and the desire for simplicity and order.'

ABOVE: The light streams into interior designer John Barman's Manhattan apartment, which has breathtaking views of the city's skyline, so in his bedroom he has had to create an area where sleep can be a priority. A wonderful charcoal grey curtain fabric by Holly Hunt has been used, and the entire room is decorated in similar tones, giving a strong yet peaceful effect. The deep pelmet is also in the same shade and creates an interesting balance with the window seat and storage area below. The curtains drop gently onto this ledge and are full enough to look soft and flowing – a difficult thing to achieve when the curtains are not full-length.

RIGHT: In a Manhattan apartment designed by Jamie Drake, a library-cum-family area has been given a warm and comfortable feel by using different tones and textures in a burnt orange colour for walls, blind, furniture and cushions, layer upon layer, creating a rich autumnal effect.

OPPOSITE: The curtain fabric in this beautiful suite at Cape Grace hotel in Cape Town was specially created by African Sketchbook for designer Kathi Weixelbaumer. The cotton hopsack was hand-painted and screen-printed in a striped effect to incorporate the three colours of the room – a pale khaki green, cream and cinnamon. The mellow shades could have been achieved, perhaps, only by painting to order, and the wonderful calligraphy on the bottom section of the drape completes the bespoke effect. The curtain, with its fold-over heading, hangs from an arrow curtain rod – the effect is stunning without being contrived.

THIS PAGE AND OPPOSITE:
Dominique Kieffer's daughter
Charlotte has transformed her
tiny Paris apartment into a little
jewel with simple yet clever ideas
– primarily, a good use of space
and making sure that every inch
counts. The fabric used for the
curtains at the French door
leading onto a small balcony is
a Dominique Kieffer fabric called
Lin Lamé in the colour Bruin,
which is a shiny, luxurious-
looking fabric with an interesting
texture. Charlotte has lined it in
an innovative way, with a very
simple Moustique linen that
creates a dramatically different
look for the curtains as seen
from the outside. Inside the
room, one gets the luxe look;
from the street, you see a simple
pure white linen. The curtain rod
is super-narrow and utilitarian,
with plain rings that do not
detract from the fabric.

BORDERS TOP TIPS

With pelmets taking more of a back seat in curtain fashions, borders can afford to be large and dramatic, although narrow borders also add a chic touch to simple drapes.

Bold borders often show a fabric in a contrasting colour or pattern, such as florals with ticking, gingham with larger checks, or wide stripes with a plain colour.

A curtain or blind can also be bordered with a fabric of a totally different weight and texture. For example, sheers can be bordered with heavy linen or cotton fabrics, silk may be combined with velvet, and wool drapes could be bordered with soft leather or suede.

Contrasting borders at the top and bottom of curtains give a neat finish and are a good way to introduce an accent colour, which can also be used for cushions and soft furnishings.

A self-border, where the main curtain fabric is doubled or tripled to make a wide border, is very effective, especially on blinds, as it gives a draped rather than a hard-edged finish.

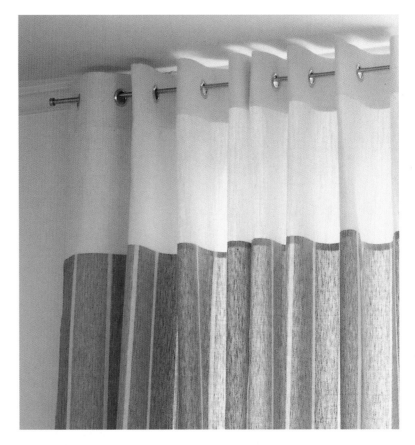

ABOVE: A large plain cream border in White Antique Linen from Roger Oates has been used here to give impact to the striped curtains, made in another Roger Oates linen called Peinture, in Raspberry. The designer has used a simple rod and eyelet heading, which has a more dramatic effect on the plain fabric border than it would have on the striped fabric.

LEFT: The curtains across the windows of this conservatory have contrasting borders along the top and bottom, with the bottom border being wider than the top. The same mustard yellow is used for the stools and cushions. A large wooden pole accentuates the almost chunky effect of the borders.

OPPOSITE: Jackye Lanham has used a chic cream all-round border to edge the thick quilt-like blue curtains in this calm, comfortable bedroom in a Florida beach house (see also pages 78–9). The fabrics are both from Travers.

CASE STUDY COMBINING FABRICS & TEXTURES

In an approach that epitomizes the new perfect curtains, a simple though rather beautiful natural fabric has been completely metamorphosed by the clever addition of a stunning border in cyclamen and khaki, which adds great impact without any apparent fussiness. The row of glass beads along the outer and lower edge of these elegant curtains adds a touch of drama.

In the living room of a suite at the Haymarket Hotel in London, designer Kit Kemp has created an extremely glamorous effect by using mainly cottons and linens rather than the more obvious choices of silks, satins and velvets. It is an unusual approach that perfectly illustrates what a little imagination and a lot of talent can bring to an interior.

For the two pairs of curtains, Kemp has used a heavy-duty cream linen from de Le Cuona, entitled Desert Cloth, which she has bordered not only with satin cotton in cyclamen pink and khaki green, but also with a row of tiny drop crystal beads along the edge to add a stunning final touch. Borders such as this are most effective and are a great way to give cream or other neutral shades additional interest and finesse. The curtains are topped with plain deep pelmets in a neutral shade of biscuit, adding a further sense of height to the already tall windows. The curtains, and indeed the entire room, retain a sense of simplicity, but with an enormous dose of glamour and pizzazz.

Another of Kit Kemp's great talents is evident here: her ability to mix several fabrics in different designs within a room in such a way that they add visual interest and surprise while creating a coherent whole. No design dominates the scheme, and the colours work together in sympathetic harmony. The two simple mirrors on the wall between the pair of curtains are the perfect touch. From every angle this room really works, achieving just the right balance of glamour, simplicity, elegance and comfort.

SWATCHES

ABOVE: Manufacturers of linen fabrics have taken enormous strides into the world of fashionable fabrics, as much in the interiors field as in clothing. Once considered a fairly informal fabric, today's linens can be used anywhere and everywhere. Available in many weights, linen looks wonderful in plain cream and off-white (5 and 7) as well as other naturals, but also comes in every colour under the sun, such as pink, cobalt and claret (2, 8 and 9). Many linen fabrics have subtle patterns in florals (1) and stripes (4), which provide a gentle way to introduce pattern, while embroidered motifs, such as cream sprigs on a green linen background (3) have a classic charm. Crinkle-effect finishes (6, 10 and 11), which are usually a cotton and linen mix and come in plains and patterns, add great texture and work well for curtains.

OPPOSITE BACKGROUND: A pale butter-coloured 100 per cent linen fabric is a ubiquitous curtain fabric in many of today's interiors.

OPPOSITE TOP LEFT: Instead of using lining fabric per se, you can use two layers of linen in contrasting colours joined together back to back, to ensure that the drapes look as good from the back as they do from the front. Here, a natural taupe linen has been backed with the same fabric in soft pale blue – the colour that would be seen through the window.

OPPOSITE TOP RIGHT: A tab-top heading is ideal if you want to hang your curtains from a wide round pole. The tabs are made in the same fabric as the main curtain, in this case a fine 100 per cent linen fabric in smart navy blue. This type of heading gives a fairly informal look.

OPPOSITE BOTTOM: I love the effect of this soft white linen fabric, which adds a new dimension to the concept of linen curtains. The special weave has vertical stitches running through it that look like grains of rice. This sample indicates how the fabric would gather and hang if a pole were slotted through the rings.

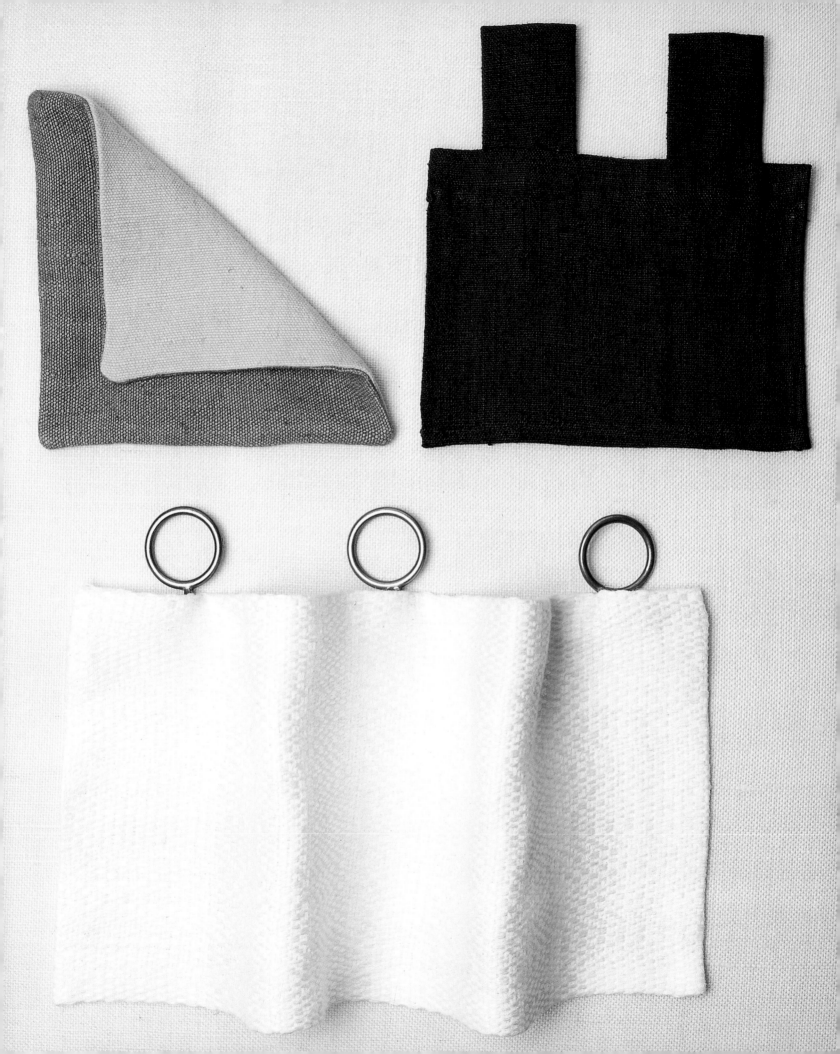

SWATCHES

ABOVE: These heavier-weight fabrics illustrate the newer, much more textured and almost tweedy weaves in pure linen, cotton and mixed compositions that have appeared on the market. Many of them have an almost wool-like effect, such as the blue/grey tweed mix (2), the thick textured taupe linen (3) and the muddy coloured pure linen herringbone (6), while other mixed compositions have an extraordinary coarse, almost mat-like texture (7). There are also more heavy self-patterned linens, such as this lovely pale grey jacquard (10) and woven stripes with wonderful texture, both horizontal (1) and vertical (8). Even the more conventionally woven plain linen fabrics (4 and 5) have a heavier feel, and can be used successfully for upholstery as well as curtains. Cotton moleskin, shown here in soft plum (9), is a good accent fabric that can be used very effectively for wide borders and narrow edgings on both curtains and blinds, as a great way to add contrasting texture.

OPPOSITE BACKGROUND: The natural weave of this medium-weight linen in heathery purple gives a wonderful depth of colour. This shade is a good neutral that would work well in many interior schemes.

OPPOSITE TOP LEFT: An unusual tweed-like heavy linen fabric has been edged with a plain linen border in the same shade of orange that appears in the main fabric. The accent colour used for a border such as this can be any of the colours featured in the tweed-like mix, and could be used elsewhere in the room, such as for scatter cushions.

OPPOSITE BOTTOM LEFT: This heavy linen in a sandy stone colour adapts well to a formal double-pleated goblet heading. This type of heading would make the fabric hang in more defined folds and would give linen curtains a structured feel.

OPPOSITE RIGHT: The silkier type of medium-weight linen, in pale grey-blue with a subtle self-pattern, hangs in soft folds when it is gathered.

The new simplicity in window treatments may be about a paring back of trimmings, elaborate pelmets and fringes that seem to overload the fabrics, but that does not mean bare, stark or insipid.

GLAMOUR

Glamour and simplicity can happily reside side by side. The fabrics are allowed to speak for themselves — and nothing says glamour, drama and sophistication better than silk and velvet.

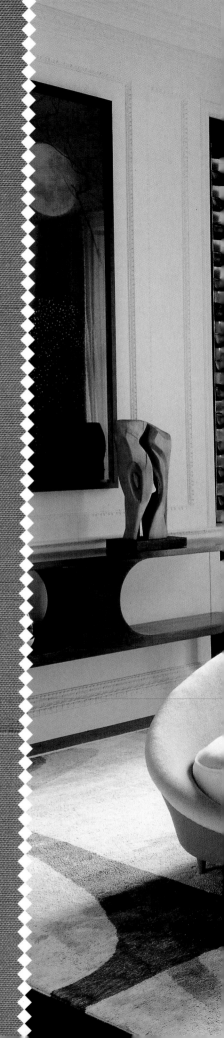

silks & velvets

Taffeta Velour Moire Silk Velvet Dupion Organza Faille Rustling Ball Gown Sumptuous Seductive Sleek Shimmering Rich Luxurious Exciting Venetian Glass Sparkling Gemstones Topaz Emerald Aquamarine Pearl Silver Moonlight

For me, 'glamour' means swathes of luscious silk, a cascade of soft, shimmering velvet, or any fabric from the legendary Italian textile house Fortuny – the epitome of luxury and sophistication, with a truly brilliant sense of refined colour. When it comes to silk, there is also the sound factor, as silk has a unique rustle that whispers 'glamour' like nothing else.

the beauty of silk

Curtains will often bring a tremendous feeling of glamour to a room – and this is not only the case with the swathes of rustling silk or cascades of sumptuous velvets that are the focus of this chapter. In many undeniably glamorous rooms, the fabrics used for curtains are simple cottons or linens, embellished or patterned sheers, or luxurious cashmere. Particularly in the case of the cottons, linens and sheers, it is the generosity of the fabric and the way in which the curtains are hung that make them exude glamour.

When typically sumptuous fabrics, such as silk, velvet, organza and faille, are used for curtains, however, the glamorous effect can be dramatically heightened. Even on the roll, these fabrics all carry a strong element of glamour; when they are hanging in generous folds from a pole, this quality becomes even more apparent.

For the ultimate in glamour, it is hard to beat silk – shantung, taffeta, plain or striped. There is something very special about its look, feel and sound that can never be equalled by any other fabric. Nothing else rustles, gleams or quite achieves the same intense depth of colour and feeling of excitement. It is a fabric that invariably adds the perfect dimension of luxe style to a room.

LEFT: This living room in an apartment in the centre of London's exclusive Mayfair has a serene elegance that makes it tranquil and very liveable. Luigi Esposito, the designer, always manages to produce stunning interiors without ever repeating himself; he uses luxury fabrics, and it shows. These curtains, with deep goblet headings, are handmade, lined and interlined. The fabric is a J Robert Scott silk called Bengaline, colour Storm. They are hung from a wall-mounted track hidden behind a slim fascia board, also covered in Bengaline. Esposito has cleverly used the same silk on the wall adjacent to the windows, giving the room a unified feel. The unlined blinds behind the curtains are a de Le Cuona fabric called Kyoto, in the colour Pewter, which has a semi-sheer pattern that is reminiscent of oil on water. They let the light filter in gently, giving a wonderful effect. One can easily see that the furniture and accessories are exquisitely chosen, and the colours throughout are muted, gentle and sophisticated.

LEFT: The glamorous curtains in the turquoise blue suite in La Residence at Franschhoek, near Cape Town, are lined pure silk taffeta with blackout sheers beneath. They have a frill as a heading and a pleated border, both made from checked blue-and-cream silk taffeta.

OPPOSITE TOP RIGHT: The stunning handmade glass pelmet designed by Andrzej Zarzycki to complement these wonderfully full silk curtains adds an extra layer of glamour to the room.

OPPOSITE BOTTOM LEFT: Goblet pleating is really effective in silk, if you require a more formal and tailored look.

OPPOSITE BOTTOM RIGHT: The overhang on the heading of these hand-painted striped curtains by African Sketchbook is wide and full, giving a quite different and very luxurious feel. This new style of heading is in keeping with the new curtain style, and provides an easy way to achieve a soft valance effect.

BELOW: The generous crumpled overhang of fabric on a tangerine silk curtain, combined with a decorative bronze pole and oversized rings, is sumptuous.

HEADINGS DOREEN SCOTT'S TIPS

When there is no pelmet or valance and the curtain heading is on full view, the workmanship must be absolutely perfect. A professional hand-sewn heading will always look best – in the same way, hems, lead edges and any trim should also be hand-sewn for the most professional finish, and to ensure that the curtain hangs well.

The heading must be the correct style for the fabric and the room in question, as well as to make your drapes look twenty-first century. A goblet or simple pleat heading are both good options, but steer clear of conventional French pleats, which can look very dated and make curtains appear instantly old-fashioned. A loose, overhanging valance is a great modern style of heading that looks both relaxed and elegant.

An eyelet heading with a 5cm (2-inch) diameter pole in nickel, chrome or burnished metal looks very contemporary. Today's lighter curtains require a less imposing pole than more structured curtains, and the way they are made enables them to concertina back fully to allow maximum light into the room when the curtains are open.

PARACHUTE SILK CURTAINS

Interior designer Jill Vantosh created this large and very elegant bathroom for her client, in which the yin-yang play of feminine and masculine, dark and light, soft and hard, unstructured and structured is evident. The open layout incorporates a generous amount of fitted storage within the dressing area, which is separated from the bathing area by means of filmy floor-to-ceiling curtains made from white parachute silk. Also used at the French doors, these gorgeous drapes soften the hard edges in the room and bring a unique airy quality to the space.

Simple blinds are often the window treatment of choice for bathrooms, in which long curtains may be affected by water and humidity. Parachute silk curtains offer a glamorous but practical alternative solution. Lightweight, absorbent and washable, they provide privacy without blocking out the light.

Fine parachute silk is ideal for use as a room divider, as it is not bulky and so does not in any way impinge on the space. This large bathroom retains its uncluttered feel and sense of openness and flow from one area to the next.

ABOVE: The simple floor-to-ceiling curtains can be drawn for privacy, to create a sense of division between the dressing and the bathing areas of this large open bathroom.

LEFT: The light and breezy swathes of diaphanous white parachute silk act as the perfect foil to the chocolate mosaic-tiled walls, dark coffee paintwork and uniform structure of the fitted storage units, introducing a soft femininity to the room, which is further reinforced by the pretty crystal chandelier.

OPPOSITE: The glamorous curtain casually draped in front of the French doors is operated by an innovative yet simple pulley system that can be used to raise and lower the curtain.

OPPOSITE: The unusual curtains in an Atlanta home interior designed by Jill Vantosh have been made from two different fabrics – a raw silk and a sheer – to give a striped effect. The curtains are hung on large wooden rings on a wooden pole, and the effect of the light streaming through the unlined fabric is beautiful against the masculine panelling.

THIS PAGE: These dramatic curtains, a combination of three different silks with a deep overhanging valance, set the stage for the decadent antique Chinese opium bed scattered with vintage cushions. The fabulous wide striped semi-sheer silk organza is from Malabar, while the claret-red silk taffeta and the divine navy-and-gold striped silk used for the heading, lining and border are from Jim Thompson. The curtains hang from plain iron rods.

design detail Even a simple curtain, when expressed in a fabric as inherently glamorous as silk, cannot fail to bring a touch of luxurious beauty to a room. An understated pleated heading can make an impact in a clean-lined contemporary setting, particularly if the ceiling is not especially high. A generous overhanging valance, on the other hand, will create a more dramatic effect, which may enhance a traditional room. Billowing folds of unlined silk have the romantic appeal of a ball gown, while the neat effect of lined and tailored silk creates a feeling of quiet elegance. Striped and plain silks can be mixed together very successfully, with contrasting linings, borders and headings, while horizontal tucks on the bottom 50cm (20 inches) of a curtain – either all the same width or increasing in size towards the bottom edge – are a truly couture touch.

'Bear in mind that pure silk is prone to fading and will deteriorate quite rapidly when exposed to strong light. A fabric with a synthetic content may be a better investment.'

OPPOSITE LEFT: The mint green frill heading and tucked border on these sumptuous, acid green silk curtains at La Residence are an inspired touch, and the green chair has wonderful bright pink embroidered flowers. This shade of acid green is my favourite and, when used with mint green and an almost Schiaparelli pink, it becomes super-special – quite stunningly over the top and the epitome of absolute glamour.

OPPOSITE RIGHT: In this soothing eating-cum-work space, light silk curtains in aquamarine blue hang simply on a specially made wire track, which is unobtrusive and perfectly functional for the flowing silk panels. The lining is another colour of the same silk – a cinnamon brown that matches the colour of the exterior walls, so that when the curtains are drawn, the walls and curtains form a seamless whole – an interesting and beautiful effect achieved very simply. The dining table is in two colours – the same ones used for the curtains. The curtains are attached by tiny ring clips to wires that protrude from painted brackets. Neither the wire nor the rings were intended for curtains, but they work well for light drapes such as these.

RIGHT: Kathi Weixelbaumer, the designer of Cape Grace hotel, turned this lobby into an enchanting vignette, with a display of blue-and-white VOC porcelain; a metal chair with a blue-and-white cloth thrown over it and lightfast pure silk dupion curtains hand-painted with calligraphy – what imagination!

One of the owners of this lovely period house in London loves light colours and contemporary detail, while the other felt that the house would benefit from a more traditional take. Interior designer Melanie Rademacher's challenge was to find a way to fuse these two concepts, to create a beautiful home that they would both enjoy.

On entering the main reception room, which stretches across the full length of the house encompassing living and dining areas, the elegant curtains make a dramatic impact, providing the room with a bold signature statement. The fabric is an oyster-coloured traditional pure silk from Bruno Triplet – New Dawn XT.06068 – which has been lined and interlined, making it stiffer and heavier than the silk usually used for curtains, especially when eyelets and poles are used. The weight allows the curtains to be very clean and tailored in style, with neat, even headings that make the fabric hang in almost military-precision folds. Had the fabric been a more flowing silk, the curtain would have dropped somewhat, and the tailored look would have not been achieved.

Eyelet headings are usually used with metal curtain poles, but, to continue the fusion between classic and contemporary, Melanie had the eyelets made large enough to move easily over traditional wide wooden poles. If the pole were narrower or metal, the effect would be lost.

The fusion of styles continues through the dining area, with a dark wood table and chairs with dark wood legs upholstered in a shade of ivory similar to the curtains. The finishing touch – another perfect compromise – is a modern chandelier that encloses a traditional candelabra.

THIS PAGE AND OPPOSITE: When I was at Hout Bay Manor hotel in Cape Town, I admired designer Boyd Ferguson's mix of grey silk and bamboo so much that I had it re-created by Doreen Scott for my living room in London. The contrast of the silk shantung in Gustavian grey against the heavy Indonesian bamboo used for the blind is an inspired choice. The silk has been doubled, rather than lined, for a lovely ball-gown effect, and the bottom section of the drapes has been pleated, with the pleats increasing in width towards the bottom edge of the curtain.

choosing silk Today, silk is available in an almost bewildering range of prices, weights, qualities and designs, so it is not hard to find the ideal fabric to enhance any space, from living area or dining room, to bedroom or bathroom. I fell in love with a window treatment designed by Boyd Ferguson for Hout Bay Manor hotel in Cape Town, which I had re-created for my drawing room (see pages 110–11). Ferguson teamed pure silk curtains with heavy bamboo blinds – an unusual and fabulous mix. For me, this captures the essence of today's innovative window treatments – the feeling that, with a good eye, everything is possible, and no combination of materials should be ruled out.

ABOVE: Striped sheer silk curtains allow light into the bedroom of this beautiful apartment in Atlanta, filled to the brim with exciting and eclectic treasures. The pleated curtains hang from just below the ceiling cornice, giving wonderful height to the room.

RIGHT: Who but Liz Biden and Ralph Krall, the designers of La Residence, in Franschhoek, near Cape Town, would have dared to team amethyst and hot pink silk on the same curtains? But this inspired colour combination really works, and the tucked border seems to truly highlight the colours and make for an even more glamorous, rustling, electric effect.

OPPOSITE: These pure silk taffeta curtains in two tones of orange are an absolute delight, especially as Liz Biden and Ralph Krall had the genius to set alongside them a large Chinese 'ancestor portrait' and an oversized armchair for two with a cushion – all in different, mouthwatering shades of orange.

THIS PAGE AND OPPOSITE: Full, heavy curtains in a silk damask by Nina Campbell for Osborne & Little, in a gorgeous amethyst/taupe shade called Purple, make a statement across the wall of windows in this elegant dining room and look wonderful in candlelight. The deep, flat, padded pelmet helps to elongate the windows and give the room height; it also hides the curtain tracks. The under-curtains are a Bruno Triplet sheer, which are hand-finished with a pinch-pleat heading and a 12.5cm (5-inch) double hem to give them weight. Interior designer Luigi Esposito has used soft tonal colours, rather than heady contrasts, with the walls in two tones of grey. The metallic backs and mauve seats of the dining chairs make a dramatic statement.

sumptuous velvet
Tactile, heavy and luxurious, velvet is another supremely glamorous fabric that is available today in a rainbow of colours, from soft neutrals to rich jewel tones, and also in many different types and weights. Until recently, I was not a huge fan of velvet being used for curtaining, as I felt it could look rather Victorian and dreary, but two factors have totally changed my mind.

First, there are the new stonewashed-effect velvets that I have seen so much of lately and which are now readily available from companies such as Andrew Martin. Their shimmering effect is infinitely more modern than the traditional, flatter-looking velvets of old, and they come in amazing colours, from pearly greys to oyster.

What is also interesting about the use of velvet fabrics today – and the second factor that has influenced me in my change of heart – is that designers such as Bernie de Le Cuona have started teaming richly coloured velvets with a backing of heavy, almost coarse woven linen, bringing an unexpected dimension to a classic fabric and giving it a new lease of life. This layering of such dramatically contrasting fabrics produces a very exciting look for a curtain.

Bear in mind that, as velvet is a heavier fabric than silk, generally these substantial drapes will require a more structured heading than lighter silk curtains, and will therefore bring a more formal look to a room.

ABOVE LEFT: Once again Andrzej Zarzycki has used that amazing glass pelmet above a traditionally designed and created lined and interlined, pleated silk curtain. The glass pelmet adds a unique sense of excitement to the room and transforms the classic curtain into an ultra-chic, elegant window dressing.

LEFT Bernie de Le Cuona demonstrates well how lining a curtain with a totally different fabric can create great drama. Here, against the background of rustic wooden floorboards, the Ruby Silk Velvet glows in a traditionally glamorous way, but then – the shock of the new – it is lined with Desert Cloth in the colour Stone, a heavily textured fabric that completely changes the effect without removing an iota of glamour.

OPPOSITE: As always, Luigi Esposito has created a supremely stylish room for this London apartment. The curtains, hanging from a covered rail, elegantly pool onto the magnificent herringbone-patterned wooden floor. The fabric is an Andrew Martin Motcomb Velvet, in a soft and superb colour called Oyster. Behind the curtains he has hung silver sheers from the Cesaro Collection by Brian Yates, which are wonderful against the Stone Lombard sofa from Andrew Martin and the chairs in Stone Linen from Bernie de Le Cuona.

I have long admired the innovative and totally desirable fabrics that Dominique Kieffer designs year after year. She is quite unique in bringing the world new ranges that are inspired by the power of her imagination and beliefs, and which owe little or nothing to the world of design around her.

Her apartment in Paris is quite ravishing – filled with her wonderful fabrics, as one would expect, with her good taste, clever ideas and inspiring *objets trouvés* evident at every turn. In this black and off-white reception room, the simply executed curtains are made of a fabulous black damask velvet – Damas Noir – a most unusual fabric that is lush, rich and theatrical. It has a very textured finish and handles really well. For additional drama, Kieffer has added a frill in black taffeta with a gold edge, Taffetas Mordoré 17107 011, which truly gives the room a 'show time' feel. The curtains hang from very simple fixtures on a plain metal rail. The effect is stunning.

This 'show time' feel contrasts exquisitely with the antique floorboards, classical white pillars and statuary, fireplace, doors and objects everywhere. The room, although dramatic in impact, is above all a welcoming and comfortable living room that perfectly illustrates how imagination when designing curtains can make such a difference to any living space. Often one finds a spectacular room that has been amazingly well designed, but that lacks soul and a feeling of comfort and cohesion. This room is most certainly not one of them – it is a triumph of truly original talent and style. The ideas are simple yet so effective, and could be applied successfully in many different settings.

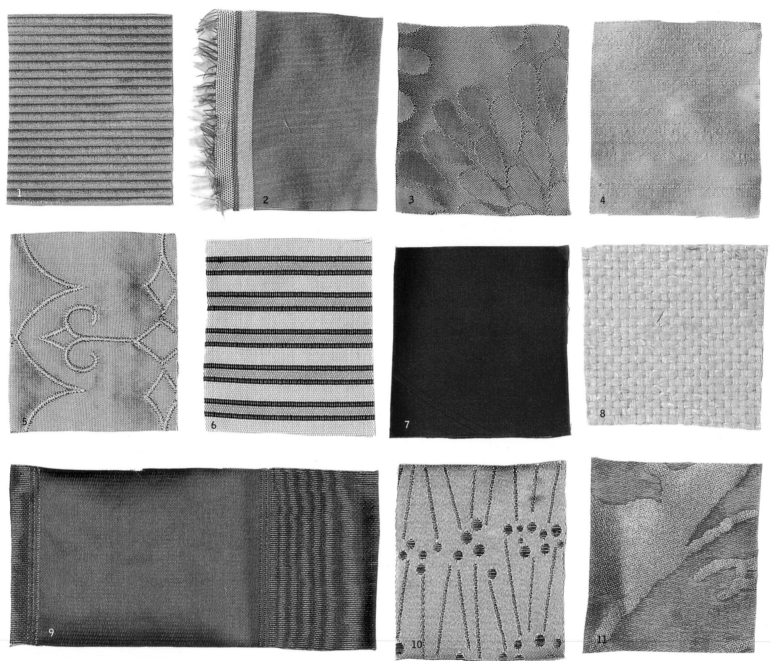

SWATCHES

ABOVE: Claremont specializes in high-end silks that are the epitome of glamour, such as the shot pink taffeta with frayed striped edge (2) and the stunning rust and bronze wide stripe (9), as well as magnificent Fortuny fabrics, such as the beautiful burnt apricot and silvery gold pattern (11). Excellent reasonably priced plain and patterned silks from the East are also available in a wide choice of colours and patterns (3 and 10). Quilted embroidered silk (5), woven silk (8) and silk taffeta with a pleated effect (12), which changes colour as the light catches it, all give very new looks, while striped silks, such as the narrow horizontal stripe in ice blue, flax and ebony (6), are true classics. Plain silk in a rich colour (7), slubby dupion silk (4) and ribbed silk-mix fabric (1) will always look chic and add a feeling of glamour to any room.

OPPOSITE BACKGROUND: Shimmery pale lilac silk would bring a beautiful touch to a feminine bedroom.

OPPOSITE TOP LEFT: Gathered in this way, Dominique Kieffer's silk taffeta Mordoré with its gold edge is perfect to use as a frill on another fabric, as on pages 118–19.

OPPOSITE TOP RIGHT: Borders, in the main fabric or a contrasting one, are very effective on soft Roman blinds. Here a berry patterned silk has been edged in Indian dupion silk in matching fuchsia.

OPPOSITE BOTTOM: Simple gathers enhance silk's luminosity, especially this gold-on-amethyst pattern.

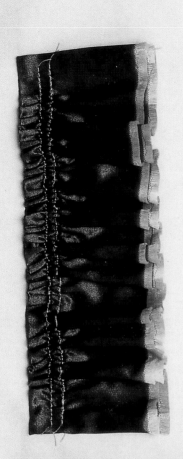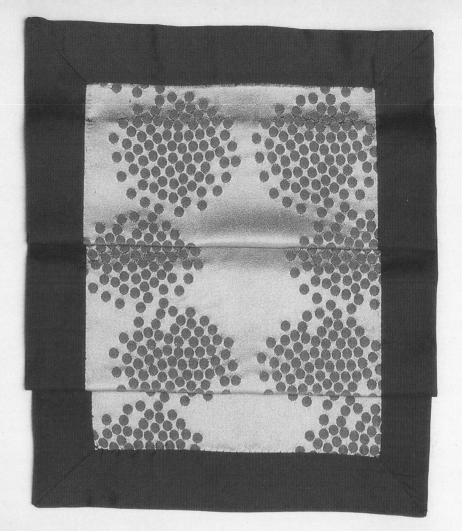

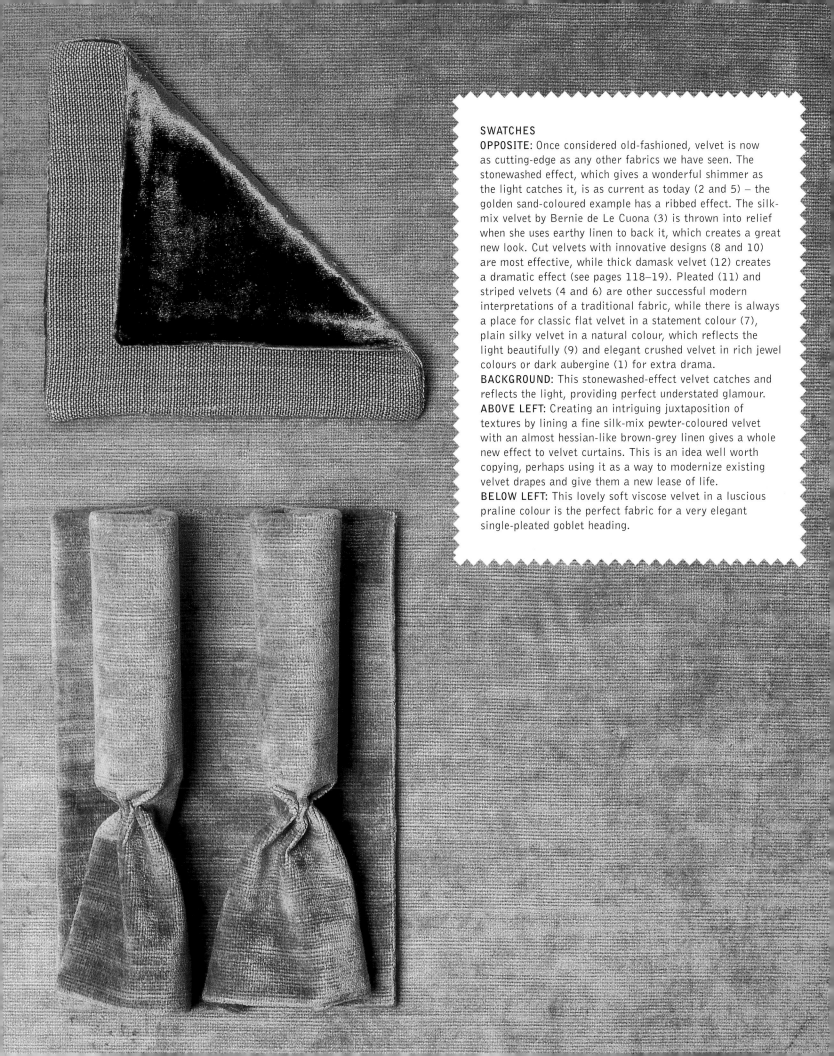

SWATCHES

OPPOSITE: Once considered old-fashioned, velvet is now as cutting-edge as any other fabrics we have seen. The stonewashed effect, which gives a wonderful shimmer as the light catches it, is as current as today (2 and 5) – the golden sand-coloured example has a ribbed effect. The silk-mix velvet by Bernie de Le Cuona (3) is thrown into relief when she uses earthy linen to back it, which creates a great new look. Cut velvets with innovative designs (8 and 10) are most effective, while thick damask velvet (12) creates a dramatic effect (see pages 118–19). Pleated (11) and striped velvets (4 and 6) are other successful modern interpretations of a traditional fabric, while there is always a place for classic flat velvet in a statement colour (7), plain silky velvet in a natural colour, which reflects the light beautifully (9) and elegant crushed velvet in rich jewel colours or dark aubergine (1) for extra drama.

BACKGROUND: This stonewashed-effect velvet catches and reflects the light, providing perfect understated glamour.

ABOVE LEFT: Creating an intriguing juxtaposition of textures by lining a fine silk-mix pewter-coloured velvet with an almost hessian-like brown-grey linen gives a whole new effect to velvet curtains. This is an idea well worth copying, perhaps using it as a way to modernize existing velvet drapes and give them a new lease of life.

BELOW LEFT: This lovely soft viscose velvet in a luscious praline colour is the perfect fabric for a very elegant single-pleated goblet heading.

Wool fabrics have an undeniable comfort factor that is hard to beat, but I had never thought of them as being in any way glamorous or sensational. Larry Laslo's stunning floor-to-ceiling

WOOL

curtains in fine bitter-coffee cashmere changed that – as did some of the new wool fabrics that I found on my travels around the world. Wool is now looking more exciting than ever before.

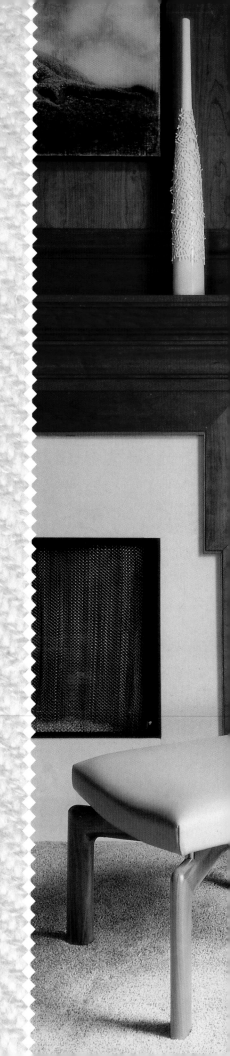

comfort zone

Cashmere Mohair Tweed Tartan Fleece Bouclé Alpaca
Paisley Chalk Stripe Prince of Wales Check Herringbone
Tactile Cosy Winter Warmth Touchy-Feely Heavy Tailored
Ski Lodge Traditional Elegant Embroidered Masculine

There are many different types, weights and textures of wool fabrics – from the softest mohair and luxurious cashmere, to traditional woven cloths. They all, without fail, bring a wonderful feeling of warmth and cosiness to an interior, and for this reason I believe wool curtains are best used in cold climates, ski lodges or rooms that get little sun.

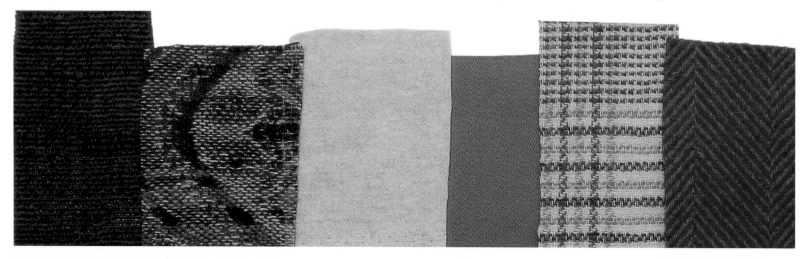

natural warmth Wool – cashmere, alpaca and mohair, as well as sheep's fleece – like so many of the natural-fibre fabrics, can have many incarnations. From the more traditional heavy woven cloths, such as plaids, tweeds and herringbones, which make highly insulating curtains, to fine wool fabrics in soft, pale colours. Wool fabric today can be as light as gossamer and as elegant as silk – and still provide a sense of enveloping warmth, to boot.

Several interior designers that I spoke to have told me that cashmere and the other heavier wool fabrics are seen more in ski chalets around the world than anywhere else – and that makes sense. These fabrics are generally at their best in cold climates and in winter when the evenings are short. There is something about the comfort factor of wool and cashmere that makes them ideal for this purpose.

BELOW AND OPPOSITE: In what designer Jackye Lanham calls her 'stone room', the wonderful curtains are made of a wool bouclé in a really rich mossy brown and hang on custom-made iron poles and rings, framing the room exquisitely. The dining chairs are upholstered in cream with brown piping, to tie in with the curtains. The iron sconces have been mounted on extra-long brackets, so that they project past the curtain returns and are not in the way when the drapes are opened or closed. This sort of specialized made-to-measure work is often what makes a room look easy, uncontrived and elegant.

USING WOOL FABRIC TOP TIPS

Wool – from heavy woven cloth to the finest cashmere – is the ideal fabric choice for curtains in cold climates and for rooms that do not get much sunshine, as it creates a feeling of cosiness as well as providing insulation.

The elegant fall of wool drapes brings a supremely soft element to a room and instantly increases the comfort factor.

If you are considering changing your curtains seasonally, wool curtains are an ideal choice for use during the winter, as they create a very different feel in a room from lightweight cotton or linen curtains that work well in the summer.

There are many lightweight wool fabrics that are worth considering for use in milder climates. These fabrics often have a proportion of silk or synthetic fibres, which gives them a lighter feel and look.

Wool fabrics generally hang well, but be aware that some of the looser weaves can drop. Stay away from the very heavy weights, too, which often do not hang as well as lighter ones.

OPPOSITE: Andrzej Zarzycki has used a fine wool fabric for these bedroom curtains, in a soft blue-grey that complements the walls and furniture. The elegantly pleated curtains hang in neat folds to the floor, giving a chic understated look. The curtain fittings are hidden under plain glass pelmets for a couture feel. A simple white blind completes the picture.

LEFT: Just as in fashion, off-white wool is supremely elegant when used in interiors. Here, Zarzycki has hung a triple-pleated curtain on a modern white-and-chrome pole with large off-white rings.

ABOVE: Luigi Esposito has used a gold mohair velvet by Donghia for these curtains, which have a beautiful hand-finished smocked heading by Emporio Interiors. Note the neat, tailored folds characteristic of lined and interlined wool. The under-curtains are a sheer from the Cesaro Collection by Brian Yates, in the colour Helios, which has a subtle gold finish that blends with the main curtains, showing a great eye for detail.

Interior designer, Andrzej Zarzycki has used lightweight wool fabrics for the two pairs of curtains in this stunning living area, which stretches from the front to the back of a traditional London town house. The tailored curtains, which are fully lined with French-pleated headings, give the room a formal yet comfortable feel that perfectly captures the mood of this elegant home.

On the side of the house that receives the most daylight and direct sunshine, Zarzycki has painted the walls and cornices a deep mahogany brown. The dark, almost black, wool curtains hang at the tall windows from large black rings on a specially ordered black pole with chrome fittings. They bring a sense of drama to the entire room.

At the other end of the same large room, which receives far less daylight and sunshine, Zarzycki has created the opposite effect. Here, cream walls and off-white skirtings are balanced by buttery cornices, while cream curtains hang from matching rings and pole.

Executed with less skill, this monochromatic scheme could have looked contrived and uncomfortable. Accomplished by an interior designer who knew just what he was trying to achieve and who took inordinate care to ensure that his clients got exactly the home they wanted, however, and the result is easy and restful. One colour flows naturally into the other, helped in part by the exemplary furnishings, artwork and objects, which all add to the fluid look of this wonderfully dramatic room.

new discoveries

In addition to traditional cloths woven in wool – the tartans, paisleys, herringbones and tweeds – there are some wonderful lighter weight wool fabrics that have a silk content. They hang well, and tend to come in paler colours, so they can be used year round, rather than just in the cooler months. Within this field are some amazing hand-woven mohair fabrics from Swaziland in southern Africa. They come in soft, light colours and great, almost ethnic patterns – the client specifies the colour and pattern, and every piece of fabric is woven and dyed to order. Coral Stephens started producing fabrics in 1947, and the company still operates in the same way, employing women in one of the poorest countries in Africa to card, spin, bobbin-wind, dye and weave these beautiful and unique high-quality fabrics for curtains all over the world.

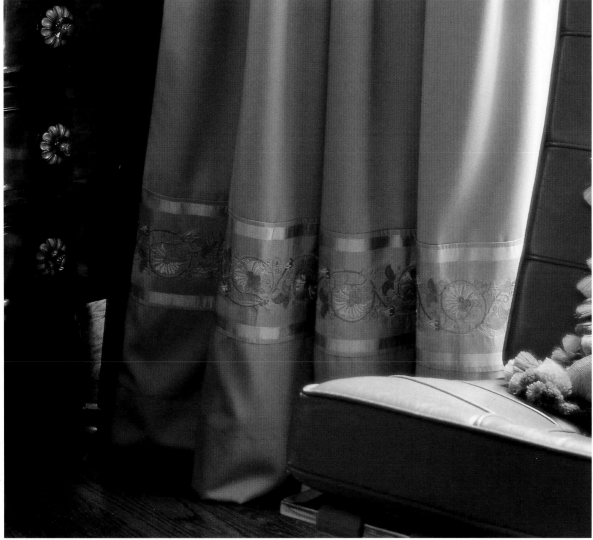

OPPOSITE: This great apartment in the former headquarters of the Atlanta chapter of the Daughters of the American Revolution is filled with more exciting and unusual furniture and accessories than I have seen assembled together in years. Accumulated with knowledge and taste, this plethora of collections forms the character of the room, and the fine wool drapes were designed as the perfect backdrop. Made by Denise Bazzuro, the elegant curtains hang on plain rods and have a felt interlining and an inverted-pleat heading. This is an ideal way to use drapes – not as a statement, but as a way of setting the scene for a dramatic room.

ABOVE: Animal-print fabrics and rugs have become a great source of neutral chic in the home. This zebra-skin rug blends beautifully with the taupe curtains and eclectic furniture.

LEFT: The clever use of an embroidered ribbon on this otherwise plain wool curtain is an excellent detail. A wide band of trim such as this can be a really effective decorative element, working as it does as an interesting but not overpowering feature.

luxurious window dressings. The curtains are very simple in style and structure, allowing the fabric itself to take centre stage, draping in beautiful soft folds down to the floor and bringing warmth and richness to this stunning yet supremely comfortable living space. The bottom third of the curtains has widely spaced hand-sewn tucks, a bespoke finish that adds an extra element of chicness. These drapes frame the windows magnificently and set the room in context, providing a perfect foil for a lifetime's collection of fine objects and art.

Behind the cashmere curtains are decorative sheer blinds with a geometric pattern. The fabric is called Fareli, in the colour Earth, and is from Laslo's new and very different range of sheer fabrics for Robert Allen (see pages 52–3). By using these sheer blinds, at one stroke Laslo has gained privacy without losing any light, and immediately injected another element of glamour into the room. As the light changes throughout the day, the patterns and effect of the shadows created change in the most fantastic way.

The entire room has been formed and structured by the soft cashmere hangings, with Laslo using a colour scheme based around their shade of dark coffee. The palette of brown tones, with just a touch of orange, gives the room a marvellous sense of calm and comfort, and proves to be the perfect neutral background for Laslo's wonderfully eclectic collection of objects, drawings and photographs. The glass, artefacts and artwork, together with the pieces of vintage as well as new furniture, all form a wonderfully homogeneous yet exciting whole.

Of all the rooms I have seen where wool has been used as curtaining, this double-height living room, in a New York town house designed by Larry Laslo, is the most chic and stunning. The curtains are the focal point of the room, enveloping the large space in a feeling of warmth, luxury and calm. The decorating scheme takes its lead from the curtains, with a colour palette based on their rich shade of brown.

Coffee-brown wool does not sound especially glamorous, but in this case it really is. Larry Laslo has used unlined finely woven cashmere at each of the tall windows, and the atmosphere created by all this sumptuous, tactile fabric evokes a sense of excitement and luxury all of its own. The curtains hang on classic hooks from thin iron poles, the severity of which only serves to accentuate the glamour of the soft,

SWATCHES

OPPOSITE: There are some wonderful sheer wools that are perfect for curtains, still giving warmth and comfort, but with an almost see-through airiness that redefines the fabric, such as the wool-and-mohair mix with coloured threads running through it (2). Other fine wool fabrics in soft patterns (4), traditional paisleys (1) and retro checks (7) bring colour to a room, and are light enough to hang softly. Pure lambswool fabric that has a satinized effect (10) is beloved by curtain makers for its light, elegant feel. Many of the other wool fabrics feel heavier and are best in colder climates or rooms used only at night, such as the classic 100 per cent wool checks in various colours (3, 8 and 9), the heavy purple wool fabric with large embroidered motifs (6), the dark brown tweed (5) and the masculine grey-and-black pinstripe (11).

BACKGROUND: The almost sheer effect of the open-weave wool-and-mohair fabric is evident; here, the ethereal cream fabric has champagne-coloured threads running through it.

TOP LEFT: Coral Stephens's 100 per cent mohair fabrics from Swaziland are dyed and woven by hand, job by job. This sample, in wonderful autumnal colours, is shown with a formal goblet pleat, but almost any heading works with these bespoke fabrics.

BELOW LEFT: A pure wool fabric patterned with faded stripes in soft modern colours is shown here with a brown moleskin border, creating an interesting mix of textures.

BELOW: Buttermilk satinized wool works in any formal heading for a simple tailored look.

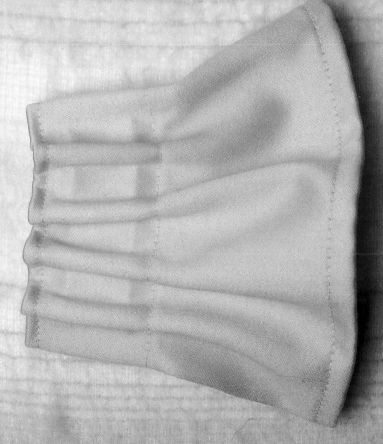

I have never been an exponent of large, bold, multicoloured patterns – either in fabric for curtains, soft furnishings or anything else – but subtle pattern, used cleverly, can add a great dimension to a room.

PATTERNS

Good fabric is expensive, and professional curtain making is also costly, so you must be really sure that you love any fabric you choose and will be happy to have it around you for years to come.

graphic

Checks Stripes Ticking Gingham Monochromatic Laser-cut Utility Ikat Retro Windowpane Check Geometric Swirls Repetition Shadow Play Brickwork Pointing Striped Ribbon Gondolier Stripes Scale Proportion Duotone Henley Stripes

Simple monochromatic, duotone or tone-on-tone patterns are, in my view, by far the easiest fabrics to live with and enjoy for many years. Graphic prints on linen, wool or silk can be smart, sophisticated or glamorous, while utility cottons such as ticking and gingham are ideal for a relaxed country style, and make great borders or linings.

geometric checks & stripes

Checked linen fabrics in soft, easy-to-live-with colours make great curtains for almost any room – from casual living rooms to elegant bedrooms. They blend well with both plain and striped fabrics, and so can provide a versatile way to mix and match patterns in similar tones. Checks come in many sizes, from very small to quite large, in solid colours or windowpane squares, and each gives a very different effect. Small and large checks in the same colour can be used in combination with each other for a change of pace – for example, a fabric with a large check can be lined or edged with a smaller check, or a small check can be used for a Roman blind under a curtain made from a larger check. Likewise, a fine sheer linen with a pattern of windowpane squares could be layered under a heavier linen patterned with solid checks of the same size and colour.

LEFT: For an interesting contrast of textures and checked pattern, Roger Oates has used his own fabric design – a viscose, polyester and cotton mix called Tristan Rouge – across this wide window, with a sheer under-curtain in 100 per cent silk called Dorabella Amethyst.

OPPOSITE: Linen curtains with a large check, both on the window and behind the bed where there is a hidden window, give a pleasing effect in this country-style bedroom designed by Jackye Lanham. The blind is in the same fabric and in the same tranquil sea-foam blue, but with a smaller check – using two sizes of check in the same colour works very well. The handmade cushions on the wooden bed are a great Lanham touch.

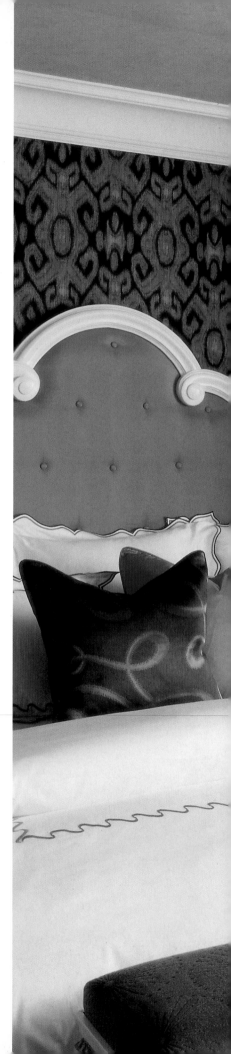

Stripes, like checks, are eternally fashionable for well-dressed interiors, but, unlike checks, stripes seem to change in style every season, becoming narrower or wider, two-coloured or multicoloured, horizontal or vertical, and even or uneven in width and spacing – the choice becomes greater with every new collection. Using a predominantly plain fabric with a thin contrasting stripe for a curtain can provide a subtle way to introduce an accent colour into an interior, which can then be repeated in artwork, cushions or other accessories. Curtains or blinds in a more dominant striped or checked pattern in a bold colour combination will make a dramatic impact on a room. The same is true when a stripe or check design features strongly contrasting colours, such as lime green with turquoise and yellow – such patterns set the scene and make a confident style statement.

ABOVE: Combining patterns, textures and tones is not easy, but here Larry Laslo has achieved an astonishingly harmonious result. Leopard print is one of his 'neutrals', and it brings the other fabrics together, in particular the striped fabric used for the blinds, Generous in Rosewood, and the sheer used for the bed curtains, Freshness in the colour Earth.

RIGHT: Laslo based his scheme for this room, at the Kips Bay Decorator Show House 2008, on an ikat fabric that he designed for Robert Allen, Quintessence in the colour Tourmaline. Based on ikat designs from Uzbekistan, it brings a vintage look to the room.

Stripes are effective in all fabrics, whether hardwearing utility cotton, fine or heavy linen, soft velvet or luscious silk. This versatile pattern seems to work universally and can be used successfully in simple crisp cotton in the most relaxed seaside cottage, through to glamorous silk in the most elegant home. Much like gingham, hardwearing cotton ticking, traditionally used to cover mattresses, can make a wonderful lining or border for a plain, checked, wider-striped or floral fabric. Another option is to create your own stripes, like Jackye Lanham of Atlanta, who joined wide strips of fabric in toning colours horizontally to create entirely original curtains (see pages 152–3).

Other geometric patterns, such as retro organic shapes or stunning ikat designs, can be very effective for a less classic look, but use them with caution, and make sure that, whatever design you choose, it is one that you truly love.

OPPOSITE: In this bedroom at the Haymarket Hotel in London designed by Kit Kemp, smart soft-hued stripes have been used on the walls and for the curtains, cushions and bed valance. The introduction of a floral fabric on the padded headboard lifts the room from a masculine feel, and this clever mix is what makes the serenely elegant bedroom work so well.

ABOVE: This room is an elegant symphony in green and cream by Jamie Drake, showcasing curtains made in one of his new fabrics designed for Schumacher. The smartly striped fabric is called Jazzed in the colour Absinthe. The turquoise glass is a typical Jamie Drake touch.

LEFT: Roger Oates has used a fabric called Antique Linen, in Rose, for the border at the top of these curtains, which have been threaded onto a slim metal pole through inset eyelets. This is a popular and simple method of hanging contemporary curtains. The colour of the border brings out the soft rose stripe in the Double Stripe linen in Rose/Teal used for the rest of the drapes.

THIS PAGE: The curtains in this drawing room designed by Jonathan Reed are in an off-white linen custom-printed in ebony brown with a pattern called Willow, designed by Albert Hadley of Parish-Hadley in New York. The 1960s graphicism works well with Reed's contemporary style. A blackened steel pole with an interesting waxed finish has been threaded through gunmetal-coloured eyelets, giving a neat, chic and well-styled effect.

OPPOSITE: Charcoal stripes have been painted onto sheer bone-coloured linen/cotton-mix fabric by African Sketchbook, giving this living room at Bishopsgrace, with its black-and-white tiled floor, an almost Venetian look. The unlined semi-sheer curtains are extremely glamorous.

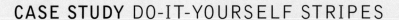
In this large family living area in a house on Sea Island in Georgia, interior designer Jackye Lanham has used striking curtains with wide horizontal stripes to set the mood. In muted earthy tones that echo the sand and sea of the surrounding landscape, the curtains are the perfect backdrop for this comfortable living room, with its magnificent view of the sea and a golf course. The addition of generous-sized sofas and armchairs, and great accent cushions and accessories in coordinating colours, makes this a perfect place to relax or to entertain as the sun goes down.

What is so interesting and innovative about this room is that the curtains, which hang floor to ceiling around two sides of the room, are actually made from three shades (03, 61 and 11) of the same Berger fabric, a sateen weave wool called 3351, which have been sewn together to form broad horizontal stripes. The neutral shades of deep duck-egg blue, creamy ivory and soft cinnamon give the entire room its decorative starting point and are reflected in the rest of the furnishings and accessories, creating a wonderful mood for the living area. The lined curtains, made by Willard Pitt, have a simple understated pinch-pleat heading that doesn't compete with the stripes for attention.

Simple rails and ironwork add a touch of class to any room. These curtains hang on elegant slim iron rods, with decorative brackets in between that add a marvellous rustic feel to the room that is perfectly in tune with the wooden beamed ceiling.

Behind the curtains are slatted bamboo blinds which, once again, are the perfect touch, adding texture to the room, as well as an Asiatic feel that is of the moment. What is really new is the juxtaposition of a rustic blind such as this with sophisticated and sumptuous fabrics – used in this way, these natural-fibre blinds, based on traditional Japanese ones, are no longer considered purely informal. I am falling in love more and more with these blinds and find that, if cleverly used, they are good in both urban and country interiors.

As always with Jackye Lanham, the furniture and accoutrements used in this room blend with fusion and synergy. The marvellous cushions with ethnic embroidery are a perfect accent, helping to bring the scheme's key colours to the furniture. The large glass bowls, the white coral and the fabrics on the furniture – by Robert Allen and Sunbrella Cello – all blend to perfection, making the room look as uncontrived and easy as if it simply grew that way.

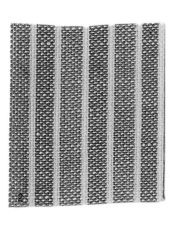

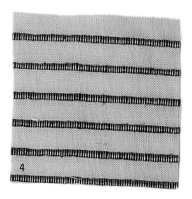

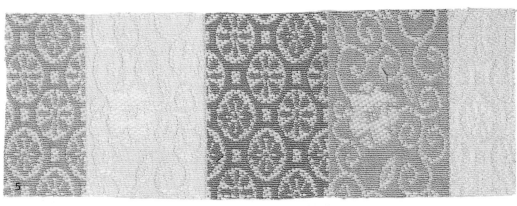

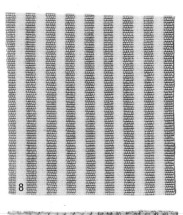

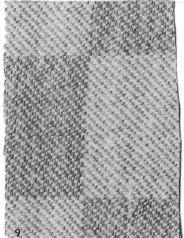

SWATCHES

LEFT: Checks and stripes offer an easy way to use pattern and are never overwhelming – it is almost impossible to make mistakes. There is a vast choice – from wide textured or patterned stripes (1 and 5) to glamorous silk (4), from chic linen-and-cotton mixes in coffee, cream and blue (2 and 6) to cosy wool that is ideal for bedrooms (9). There are also the ubiquitous gingham checks and simple stripes in various sizes and weights (3, 7 and 8) that are great in beach houses, country homes, kitchens and bathrooms.

OPPOSITE BACKGROUND: Medium-weight cotton gingham in beige and biscuit could be used to back another neutral fabric.

OPPOSITE TOP LEFT: Simple box pleats on a chic blue linen-and-cotton mix crisscrossed with cream threads demonstrates an idea for a valance for cream or navy drapes.

OPPOSITE BOTTOM LEFT: A mini check in cream and blue and a wide stripe in cream and seafoam illustrate how checks and stripes can be combined for a border, with the seam hidden by a cream textured braid.

OPPOSITE RIGHT: Blue cotton moleskin has been used to edge a cream cotton fabric with narrow stripes in two shades of blue – a great effect for a curtain or blind.

OPPOSITE: In principle, I am not very fond of large floral designs, so I should have hated this room in the Haymarket Hotel in London – in fact, I loved it. Kit Kemp has broken every rule in my book and succeeded in created a stunning and memorable interior. The wonderful curtains are in Christopher Farr's linen fabric Peonies, in a shade of pink to end all pinks. I even love the shaped pelmet with its contrast edging, which has an Indian Moghul feel. When juxtaposed with the stonewashed pink sofa – upholstered in a fabric by Romo – the result is quite wonderful. All the other pink elements in the room – pictures, lamps, chair and cushions – combine to make this a room to remember.

**SWATCHES
BELOW, LEFT TO RIGHT:**
An Indochine-inspired floral design on a cotton-and-linen-mix fabric (see pages 162–3); indigo rose on natural pure linen; bleached linen with delicate cherry blossom design; cotton-and-linen mix French toile in raspberry; stone-coloured linen with a French floral design in cream.

florals & pictorials

Roses Peonies Anemones Lilies Tulips Hydrangeas Tea Roses
Bold Blooms Delicate Sprigs Bouquets Foliage Garlands Imari
Compagnie des Indes Faded Chintz Jacquard Tone on Tone
Damask Coral Calligraphy Toile de Jouy Butterflies Bees

Traditional prints such as chintz, cottage-garden florals and toile de Jouy have an enduring appeal that transcends fashion, but it is the new antique-looking fabrics in subtle mono- or duotones that look the most modern and elegant, while hand-painted calligraphy and pictorial designs bring a new and exciting dimension to patterned fabrics.

the floral renaissance

Floral linens and cottons have, for many years, been staple design elements, particularly where curtains are concerned. Wonderful traditional designs from old documents, pattern books and pieces of fabric were redrawn, recoloured or reinvented to bring a host of large and colourful bequests into the drawing rooms of the world. These floral designs were the mainstay of the English Country House style, although many of the more beautiful of these designs were French in origin – and Indochine in style, based on the traditional chintz that was introduced to the West during the seventeenth century.

While there are, of course, many traditional vibrant and colourful floral fabrics to be found – from country garden blooms such as rambling cabbage roses, overblown peonies and bold tulips, to sweet sprigs and delicate branches of cherry blossom – in recent years this ubiquitous look has undergone a considerable metamorphosis.

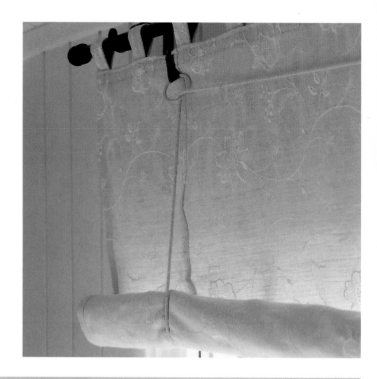

ABOVE: This kitchen blind, in a cabin in Norway interior designed by Helene Forbes-Hennie, is a cream linen fabric embroidered with a floral design, also in cream – a subtle way to introduce pattern into a small space.

LEFT AND OPPOSITE: The triple-pleated heading shows off the delightful Chelsea Editions green floral fabric that has been used for the deep borders on the top and bottom of these Fabricut ivory linen curtains, finished to perfection by the green piping. Jackye Lanham and her curtain maker Willard Pitt are past masters at this sort of detailed finish that makes all the difference to the look of a room. The iron pole from Atlanta's Palace Forge is beautiful, with its decorative finial and deep hooks. The drapes work well with the soft cream tones used in this large bedroom. The framed bone necklaces are a lovely touch.

OPPOSITE AND BELOW: The vintage-looking floral pattern on the Parnham Blue linen fabric was adapted from an original document by Annie Dubbs, who designed this range of fabrics for Blithfield & Co. Light streams through the windows of this large bedroom in a stunning Manhattan apartment, and the curtains with their simple gathered heading, together with the light furniture, add to the sense of peace.

RIGHT: Cabbages & Roses fabrics are also vintage in style and based on archive prints that the designer Christina Strutt finds and adapts. These curtains are made from its Tulips and Roses fabric and hang in a simple fashion from an antique brass pole on antique brass hooks.

BELOW RIGHT: Interestingly, this Cabbages & Roses fabric – called Cerise Hatley – is printed directly onto antique linen, so it has a truly authentic vintage look. It is a wonderful fabric to use with antique furniture and gives a perfect country-cottage feel.

FADED FLORALS TOP TIPS

For the best vintage effect, choose muted florals in soft, subdued palettes, such as any of the fabrics by Cabbages & Roses, whose 'faded' colours give a very authentic timeworn look.

Faded florals work especially well in country cottages or homes with an informal 'shabby chic' style, while bold overscaled florals can bring a welcome splash of colour and pattern to contemporary interiors. Classic chintz patterns can seem a little old-fashioned, but often work well in traditional interiors.

When making curtains with patterned fabric, remember that all cut lengths have to start at the same point in the pattern, so that they match at the seams when they are joined.

Where large patterns are used, it is better to have a full pattern at the hemline and a part pattern in the heading where it is less noticeable.

ABOVE AND RIGHT: This mellow living room has been decorated by Christina Strutt in Cabbages & Roses fabrics in summer fruit colours. The curtains are made in India Rose – a great adaptation of an Indochine fabric – and are hung from large white rings on a white wooden pole, falling softly into a puddle on the floor. The red cushions are in Raspberry French Toile; the bolster is in India Rose.

faded florals In addition to some exceptional floral designs, including stunning bold monochromatics and, at the other end of the scale, subtle damasks that have an enduring classic appeal, the floral fabrics that really stand out from the crowd are the plethora of beautiful faded prints that have been artificially aged to make them look antique or vintage. These seemingly timeworn, sun-bleached patterns bring a whimsical sense of romance to an interior, as well as a reassuring lived-in feel. There is nothing twee or saccharine about these faded florals: they are elegant, sophisticated and timeless. In soft, almost dirty colours, often on a warm cream, pale taupe or grey background, they work as well in pared-back interiors, with stripped or painted floorboards and contemporary furniture, as they do in more traditional antique-filled homes.

Small independent companies, such as Brocante, Elanbach, Cabbages & Roses and Ernest & Matilda, are bringing new fabric collections onto the market all the time, reproducing and reinventing wonderful, elegant archive prints – usually on linen rather than cotton, but not always. I have included many of these designers and manufacturers in the Resources list on page 188, and I recommend that you look at their collections and do your research well before making a floral choice, as there are lovely new designs being produced every season.

'Faded florals give a room a whimsical sense of romance, as well as a reassuring lived-in feel.'

LEFT AND OPPOSITE: A very different curtain style has been designed by Kit Kemp for this bedroom in London's Haymarket Hotel. Two fabrics have been combined in an innovative way, adding height to the room, as well as exciting pattern and colour. The covered curtain rail is mounted well above the window, and the deep French-pleated valance in the striped fabric Chicago, from Kvadrat, hangs from it, falling softly over the multicoloured flower print, Designers Guild's Rosales Parma. The raspberry pink sofa in front of the window, in Kvadrat's Happy, provides the perfect focus for the room and adds a supremely comfortable feel.

THIS PAGE: In this comfortable guest bedroom in a Sea Island home, Jackye Lanham used a pink and khaki fabric by Osborne & Little for the curtain pelmet and border, bed curtains and stool. The main part of the drapes and the back of the bed curtains are in a fabric called Koeppel-style Chinon in the colour Eggshell.

THIS PAGE: The hemp and linen curtains in a master bedroom designed by Jonathan Reed have been hand-printed by Opuzen in a dark walnut colour on a natural ground, in a design called La Scala. The cylindrical pleating of the curtain heading is known as cartridge style, and the curtains are hung on ebony painted wooden poles. The daybed in front of the curtains, in three natural tones of cinnamon, rust and cream, harmonizes well.

THIS PAGE: African Sketchbook hand-painted each drop of these coral-patterned curtains for the living room of Hout Bay Manor hotel in Cape Town, designed by Boyd Ferguson. The curtains hang from a heavy wooden pole over a bamboo blind, and pool onto the carpet.

RIGHT: Authentic reproductions of blue-and-white VOC porcelain plates were painstakingly painted onto these curtains made of silk dupion by African Sketchbook. There are no images on the fall-forward of the overhanging heading, or too close to the hem – something that could be achieved only by hand, drape by drape. The silk dupion is resistant to light – an innovative breakthrough for all those who have despaired when their silk curtains began to fade around the edges.

BELOW: I love this style of curtain, where the fabric continues above the heading and falls forwards over the top edge of the curtain, forming a simple but extremely effective quasi-valance that is innovative and contemporary, yet still works well in a traditional room. The 100 per cent cotton hopsack was first hand-painted with a crunchy white wash and then screen-printed with the 1651 VOC mandate given to Jan van Riebeeck to establish Cape Town as a refreshment station.

pictorial pattern
A far cry from traditional pictorial designs such as toile de Jouy, with its gentle pastoral scenes – or even its more modern, edgy reinterpretations that depict gritty tales of urban life – are the unusual hand-painted designs from a small eco-friendly company in Cape Town. African Sketchbook Fine Art Fabrics employs local craftsmen to produce stunning hand-painted silk, velvet, cotton and linen for curtains. Each drape is made to order, in the colour and design desired by the client. Almost anything is available for the asking, from a curtain in a specially dyed colour-matched fabric, to a document from a French chateau. The pattern requested is always perfectly matched curtain by curtain, as each one is painted individually. The company even offers fadeproof silk – something new to me. Particularly stunning were the silk curtains painted with calligraphy from seventeenth-century documents, which would work wonderfully in almost any scheme and bring a feeling of history to a home.

a room appeared, and the fabric was the perfect colour and design, with yardage enough.

From this simple beginning emerged this enchanting room – a pretty guest bedroom in a charming beach house. The lavender fabric gives an intimate and unusual twist to the room, making the guest, I am sure, feel special and pampered. A display of Swedish plates on one wall, collected over a long period of time, together with the purple glass bottles beneath, found on a scouting visit to Jacksonville in Florida, tie in with the colour scheme beautifully and give the room a unified feel.

The bed curtains are made from a delicately embroidered voile and have a lovely smocked heading, which adds great detail. They are simply tied onto the iron bed frame with lavender-coloured satin ribbons for a very pretty, feminine effect. These bed curtains are perfect – not at all claustrophobic, but rather giving a light, soft and airy feeling to the bed and indeed to the room. The same curtains hang over the closets instead of doors – conventional cupboards would have made the room feel too crowded, as there is little space for doors to open.

The patterned curtains that started this story hang at the windows from a simple iron pole with a very Lanham touch – large iron rings, which contrast well with the softly coloured and patterned fabric that dictated the fresh, feminine scheme for this bedroom. The buttons that adorn the curtains 'fastening' each pleat – another of Lanham's signatures – give a truly couture feeling to the curtains and add to the great attention to detail evident in this sweet room, in which every aspect has been carefully thought out and executed.

This lavender blue guest bedroom at designer Jackye Lanham's beach house is a wonderful example of a sort of serendipity and a philosophy that I really believe in – buy something that you fall in love with and wait until you find the perfect use for it. When it comes to fabric, this can often produce far more pleasing and successful results than looking for what you want when you want it. The same principle applies to clothes shopping – you always find the perfect outfit when you don't need it.

Jackye Lanham saw the floral-patterned fabric used for these curtains in a small shop selling ceramics and other pretty objects when on holiday in Italy. She had no particular plans for it and realized that the yardage was not much, so decided to keep it until she found the perfect room for it, one with not very large windows. Eventually such

SWATCHES

OPPOSITE: Today's most notable florals seem to divide into two very clear groups. The first is characterized by faded, often archival prints on natural pure linen or linen-mix backgrounds, whose seemingly sun-bleached colours form a tranquil backdrop that is easy to live with (1 and 3). There is also the wonderful classic floral hand-painted in muddy colours onto a linen-and-cotton-mix sheer (7). These fabrics all lend themselves to use with vintage furniture in classic country-style rooms. The other group of florals tend to be duotone prints – cream and a main colour (2, 4, 5 and 6). Stronger and more defined, they are more conducive to use in contemporary rooms.

BACKGROUND: This fine natural cotton-and-linen-mix fabric features a charming archival print in a soft almost dirty blue. This is an elegant floral that would work well in a living room or bedroom.

LEFT: A classic country-garden floral illustrates how effective it can be to use interesting buttons across a curtain heading, making sure that a button is placed centrally on each pleat.

BELOW LEFT: A pretty antique-look floral linen has been lightly gathered and edged with a toning blue fabric, illustrating how a plain heading with narrow ties can be used to hang a light curtain for an informal, feminine look.

BELOW: The soft vintage feel of this beautiful lavender floral on a natural linen background is accentuated by the addition of a narrow linen border in a stronger toning colour.

One of the most interesting and dramatic changes that has taken place in recent years in interior style is that it is no longer obligatory to have curtains at windows as a matter of course.

OTHER MATERIALS

New technology and the development of new materials have brought other practical and exciting options to the forefront of designers' imaginations.

BELOW: The chain mail used by John Barman at this window of his Manhattan apartment is an imaginative choice of material and most effective in an urban setting. It can also be used successfully as a cover for large heating units. This chain mail is from Barry London Glass and Shade in New York City.

alternatives to curtains

Screens, shutters, panels and blinds are available in many different styles and materials, from wood and natural fibres such as bamboo and seagrass, to plastic and metal. What you choose will depend on your interior style and the type of effect you wish to create. Wooden plantation shutters, stripped, stained or painted, filter the light in interesting ways, creating plays of light and shadow. They can be full-height or half-height, letting in light but retaining privacy, and suit traditional and contemporary interiors alike. Panelled shutters will block out the light entirely, so they can be a good choice for a bedroom where total darkness is required. Cutting-edge screens and window coverings made from metal or plastic will probably work best in modern settings, as their effect is likely to be too harsh for traditional interiors.

ABOVE: The use of this futuristic mirrored screen across the windows of his skyscraper apartment was a stroke of genius by John Barman. The screen is the focal point of the room and adds great light and depth to the interior. In contemporary surroundings such as this, unusual materials work exceptionally well as a replacement for curtains. Bravo!

THIS PAGE: In this dining room by Mimmi O'Connell, the eye is immediately drawn to the vintage bamboo blinds from Borneo, juxtaposed to great effect with a collection of woven baskets. Behind is a simple sheer blind. The table is covered with vintage Welsh quilts in a magnificent orangey red. This lovely room, with oriental flair, works as well with a few diners as it does with many.

OPPOSITE TOP AND BOTTOM LEFT: The kitchen blind in a home in Atlanta designed by Tim Hobby is made of paper and cut to measure for the shaped window. The grass-effect material is very attractive, and the bespoke shape adds an element of chic.

OPPOSITE BOTTOM RIGHT: A curtain makes a great room divider for a multifunctional space. In this case, interior designer Jonathan Reed has added another dimension by making the curtain out of panels of calf leather with a topstitch detail and lining it in cashmere – the height of luxury and glamour. The heading is an eyelet one and the chic pole is blackened steel.

Natural-fibre blinds made from bamboo, banana fibre, jute, rattan or seagrass are a new and very exciting addition to the range of window treatments that are being widely used to such good effect in interiors around the world. They are a great neutral, and used on their own they bring a natural, earthy rustic feel to a room; however, when layered with curtains in dramatically contrasting textures, they create a fabulously different look. When teamed with billowy silk or decorative sheers, for example, the effect is über-glamorous; paired with wool sateen or tailored linen, the look is sophisticated and Zen-like. This is, without doubt, a new and interesting way of dealing with windows.

Of course, another option is to have no window treatment at all. If privacy is not an issue – for example, if you live in a high-rise or on the waterfront and are not overlooked – consider leaving windows bare: the view is all.

As with fabrics, the range of poles, finials, hooks and various other curtain paraphernalia has grown enormously, and there are now many different styles available, both off-the-shelf and custom-made.

HARDWARE

The style you choose is largely down to personal taste, although any hardware should complement your curtains and not detract from them – remember, it is the curtain that should take centre stage.

curtain considerations

Having a set of drapes made by a curtain maker can be both daunting and costly. As we have seen, there has never been anything like the selection of fabrics – colours, designs and strange and wonderful composites – as that which exists today. It is hard for an expert to choose, so it can be staggeringly difficult for an amateur. I hope that the many different types of curtains and fabrics illustrated in the previous chapters will be of some assistance in aiding you to make an informed decision, but I want to mention another alternative.

Ready-made curtains may have been dull and ordinary a decade ago, but many companies are now producing exciting and innovative ranges. The advantage of ready-made curtains is that you know exactly what you are getting before you buy, so there are no surprises. In the UK,

PREVIOUS PAGE: Two parallel curtains hang at each window in Mimmi O'Connell's living room (see also pages 74–5). The two layers, in cream pure linen by John England, run on separate iron rods by means of iron curtain eyelets, so that they can be drawn individually to create different looks. This contemporary style is simple but dramatic, and perfect for any interior. Both the hand-forged steel poles and the bracket have a waxed finish, and are from the Bradley Collection.

LEFT: These flat panels by Silent Gliss can be moved and arranged in many different ways, and can be used with curtains or instead of them at windows, or as room dividers. The panels can be plain or patterned fabric in various colours, to give different effects, and are great for modern homes with large expanses of glazing. This example is Panel Glide in a Kvadrat fabric called Nectar.

OPPOSITE: In the breakfast room of Bishopsgrace hotel in Cape Town, designer Kathi Weixelbaumer has draped sheer curtains over the poles and used groups of unusual curtain clips in the shape of treble clefs to hold the fabric in place. These breezy sheers allow in light, but retain privacy, and each full drop of fabric has a large hand-embroidered 'BG' monogram.

John Lewis stores offer a great selection of ready-made curtains; French company Blanc d'Ivoire has a fabulous range of silks, velvets and sheers that gets more ambitious every year; IKEA sells ready-made curtains with a typically Scandinavian aesthetic; and in the USA companies such as West Elm, Martha Stewart, Ethan Allen, Crate & Barrel and Williams-Sonoma all produce exceptional ready-made curtains. Many of these suppliers also produce great curtain rods, hooks and tiebacks – and provide helpful advice.

Skimpy-looking curtains are unattractive, so be generous with ready-made curtains to guarantee a couture feel – an extra curtain on each side can make a huge difference. Consider using combinations of curtains for a layered look, and choose curtains with borders, or customize them. Be ambitious and innovative, and success will be yours.

TOP LEFT: The tones of cognac, platinum, zarin, graphite and champagne make up the subtle sheen of the luxurious metallic finish of these pared-down modernist poles and finials. The temple-shaped finials come in two sizes – 30mm (1³⁄₁₆ inches) and 50mm (2 inches) diameter.

TOP RIGHT: These beehive-shaped finials in a flat silver gilt finish have a contemporary twist. They are available in 50mm (2 inches) and 63mm (2.5 inches) diameter, and have a matching tieback (shown on the left).

ABOVE LEFT: There are many reproductions of traditional finials, and this spiral ball design in a dull brass finish is an elegant example. The smaller finial is 50mm (2 inches) and the larger one is 63mm (2.5 inches) in diameter.

ABOVE RIGHT: This black Shagreen Cone finial has a streamlined shape that would suit a modern interior.

OPPOSITE BOTTOM LEFT: Solid-looking incised bracelet rings on a chunky pole in a metallic finish create an industrial feel, and would be ideal for curtains made in a heavy fabric.

poles, finials, hooks & rings

Manufacturers are now producing a wide range of interesting and attractive curtain hardware – poles, rods, tracks, hooks, rings and finials – in many different styles and materials, from traditional wood and various types of metal, including steel, chrome and iron, to contemporary glass and acrylic. My favourite iron and steel rods are available from the Bradley Collection in the UK and Palace Forge in the USA. There are also companies, such as McKinney & Co., that make ideas and concepts a reality with their made-to-measure curtain rails and rings. Plain iron rods and rings can also be commissioned from local artisans and blacksmiths.

Increasing in popularity for hanging very light, sheer curtains is a minimal, almost barely-there industrial look, where the fittings are virtually invisible and are the type that can be bought from a hardware store, as well as from a specialist curtain supplier. Instead of a traditional pole, a very thin rod or tensioned wire is attached to the wall with an industrial-style fitting. The rings used can also be bought from a hardware store.

ABOVE: An unusual pepper-mill-shaped finial is shown here in four different finishes. Make sure that the finish you choose, as well as the shape and style of the finial, will complement your choice of fabric and not overpower it.

BELOW: Different finishes can create very different effects, as demonstrated by this selection of poles and finials. The top two examples have decorative spiked-ball finials on bamboo- and tortoiseshell-effect poles. The ivory carved wooden pole with matching rings is very chic, and would work well with any fabric, as would the simple limed-oak pole and finial (bottom).

In recent years, the eyelet-and-pole option has been refined and customized, so that eyelets can now be purchased in many different sizes and finishes. The gunmetal and iron finishes, in particular, give a very new and contemporary look. Dark eyelets with an iron pole work well on pale linen curtains. A double pole, held by brackets, is practical as well as attractive, allowing two curtains to be hung one in front of the other, so that different effects can be achieved depending on how far each curtain is pulled. The key is to leave enough space between the poles for the curtains to move easily, but not so much that they protrude from the wall in an obtrusive manner.

Tim Hobby of Atlanta showed us how curtains can work on mechanical systems (see pages 32–3). These are growing in popularity, particularly with people who like gadgets and machinery. I, however, would be sure to make the taps run hot water when I think that I am closing the drapes. For a mechanical system to be a success, someone in the household has to be computer- and mechanically minded, otherwise it can be a potential recipe for disaster.

LEFT: Chrome and acrylic poles, rings and finials are good choices for contemporary rooms. The simpler they are, the more they are in keeping with a paired-back modern look, and acrylic rings are particularly attractive. These examples are, top to bottom, acrylic pole and finial with dark nickel fittings and trim; stainless-steel pole with a rounded acrylic finial; polished-steel pole and flat-ended finial – the finish has a lead-like appearance; acrylic pole and matching rings with sleek chrome finial; polished steel with spiral pointed finial.

OPPOSITE TOP LEFT: Simple tensioned wires attached to the wall with industrial-style brackets are good choices for hanging sheers. A stand-off allows tension-wire systems to work around corners or bay windows.

OPPOSITE TOP RIGHT: When interior designer Melanie Rademacher and curtain designer Doreen Scott created an eyelet-heading curtain to go around the corners of a bay window, they collaborated with a craftsman to devise a way of achieving this with a special rod and a new type of bracket (see also pages 18, 21 and 108–9). As long as there are people with imagination and craftsmen with ingenuity, new innovations of this nature will continue to happen in the field of curtain design.

OPPOSITE BOTTOM LEFT: Curtain hooks with a difference, these rustic iron treble clefs attach long floor-to-ceiling drops of sheer cotton in the charming breakfast area in Bishopsgrace hotel in Cape Town. Practical, imaginative and elegant, the clips anchor the panels in place, demonstrating a very different way of hanging curtains.

OPPOSITE BOTTOM RIGHT: A strip of mirror has been attached to the wall behind the curtain heading to give the effect of a double curtain. What a simple idea, and yet what a magical effect it gives.

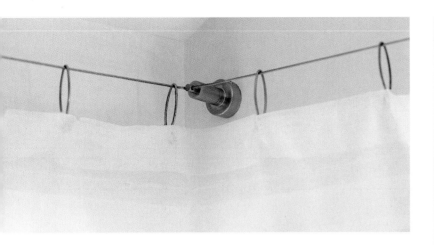

CHOOSING POLES MELANIE RADEMACHER

Curtains set the mood for the room, but the choice of pole is an important element. A dark, chunky wooden pole (or any other dark or contrast-coloured pole) will draw the eye up. Make sure that you go for a thick one — at least 4–5cm (1½–2 inches) diameter — as otherwise the effect will be lost.

Side brackets are generally hidden by the curtains, but choose good-quality ones, as they will be stronger.

The finial at the end of the pole is what sets the style — wooden or painted finials can create a traditional feel, while glass or acrylic gives the wooden pole a contemporary edge.

Your choice of pole should complement the style of curtain, but it is the drape that should take centre stage. A simple white pole is a good neutral choice and will let your curtains grab the attention. You can make it a little more exciting in a modern white environment with chrome brackets and rings.

Resources

Fabricut, OK
t +1 800 999 8200
www.fabricut.com

Galbraith & Paul, PA
t +1 215 508 0800
www.galbraithandpaul.com

Gracious Home, NY
t +1 800 338 7809
www.gracioushome.com

Greentex Upholstery Supplies
Inc, NY
t +1 800 762 8303
www.greentexinc.com

Gretchen Bellinger Inc., NY
t +1 518 445 2400
www.gretchenbellinger.com

S Harris, OK
t +1 800 999 5600
www.sharris.com

Highland Court, NY
t +1 631 273 8800
www.highlandcourtfabrics.com

Holly Hunt, IL
t +1 800 320 3145
www.cowtan.com

Home Tex Fashions Inc., MN
t +1 800 328 2437
www.hometexfashions.com

Jessitt Gold, CA
www.jessittgold.com

Joseph Noble, TX
t +1 214 741 8100
www.josephnoble.com

Knoll Inc., PA
t +1 877 615 6655/
1 800 343 5665
www.knolltextiles.com

Kravet, NY
t +1 888 891 4112
www.kravetcontract.com

J Lambeth & Co. Inc., WA
t +1 202 646 1774
www.jlambeth.com

Lee Jofa, NY
t +1 888 533 5632
www.leejofa.com

Lulan Artisans, SC
t +1 843 722 0118
www.lulan.com

Luna Textiles, CA
t +1 415 252 7125
www.lunatextiles.com

Maharam, NY
t +1 800 645 3943
www.maharam.com

Metro Mills Inc., NY
t +1 973 942 8885
www.metromillsinc.com

Mitchell Fabrics, IL
t +1 800 447 0952
www.mitchellfabrics.com

Opuzen Design, CA
t +1 323 549 3489
www.opuzen.com

Pallas Textiles, WI
t +1 800 472 5527
www.pallastextiles.com

Pasini Pelle, FL
t +1 415 674 6773
www.pasinipelle.com

Peter Fasano, MA
t +1 413 528 6872
www.peterfasano.com

Pindler & Pindler Inc., CA
t +1 805 531 9090
www.pindler.com

Pollack, NY
t +1 212 627 7766
www.pollackassociates.com

Ralph Lauren Home, USA
t +1 888 475 7674
www.ralphlaurenhome.com

Randolph & Hein, NY
t +1 212 546 9001
www.randolphhein.com

Robert Allan, Massachusetts, MA
t +1 800 333 3777
www.robertallandesign.com

J Robert Scott, CA
t +1 877 207 5130/800 322 4910
www.jrobertscott.com

Rodolph Fabrics, CA
t +1 707 935 0316
www.rodolph.com

Rogers & Goffigon Ltd, CT
t +1 203 532 8068

Sanderson, NY
t +1 800 894 6185
www.sanderson-uk.com

Scalamandre, NY
t +1 631 467 8800
www.scalamandre.com

F Schumacher & Co., NY
t +1 800 862 3011
www.fschumacher.com

Silk Dynasty Inc., CA
t +1 650 903 0078
www.silkdynasty.com

Sina Pearson Textiles, NY
t +1 212 366 1146
www.sinapearson.com

Summerhill Ltd, NY
t +1 212 935 6376
www.summerhill.com

Texstyle, NJ
t +1 201 358 8333

Travers & Co., NY
t +1 212 888 7900

Tylergraphic, NY
f +1 212 924 6693
www.tylergraphic.com

Westgate Interiors, SC
t +1 800 527 6666
www.westgatefabrics.com

Yoma Textiles, NY
t +1 212 431 4794
www.yoma.com

FABRICS FRANCE
Autrefois Claire Puyala, Poussan
t +33 (0)4 67 78 42 04
www.autrefois-clairepuyala.com

Belinac, Saint Etienne
t +33 (0)4 77 43 37 00
www.belinac.com

Casamance, Willems
t +33 (0)3 20 61 72 22
www.casamance.com

Charles Burger, Paris
t +33 (0)1 42 97 46 19
www.charles-burger.fr

Creation Baumann, Paris
t +33 (0)1 45 49 08 22
www.creationbaumann.com

Creations Metaphores, Paris
t +33 (0)1 44 55 37 00
www.creations-metaphores.com

Dominique Kieffer, Paris
t +33 (0)1 42 21 32 44
www.dkieffer.com

Dominique Picquier, Paris
t +33 (0)1 42 72 23 32
www.dominiquepicquier.com

Edmond Petit, Paris
t +33 (0)1 40 13 83
www.edmond-petit.com

Elitis, Toulouse
t +33 561 80 20 20
www.elitis.fr

Elodie Brunet, Paris
t +33 (0)1 53 59 90 26
www.elodiebrunet.com

Karin Sajo, Paris
t +33 (0)1 46 06 82 16
www.karinsajo.com

Lelievre, Paris
t +33 (0)1 43 16 88 00
www.lelievre.tm.fr

Manuel Canovas, Paris
t +33 (0)1 40 51 95 30
www.manuelcanovas.com

MM Design
t +33 (0)6 16 68 04 72
www.mmdesign1.com

Mokuba, Paris
t +33 (0)1 40 13 81 41
www.mokuba.fr

Pierre Frey, Paris
t +33 (0)1 44 47 36 00
www.pierrefrey.com

Toiles de Mayenne, Fontaine-Daniel
t +33 (0)2 43 00 34 80
www.toiles-de-mayenne.com

Veraseta, Paris
t +33 (0)1 42 97 52 62
www.veraseta.fr

FABRICS – ITALY
C & C Milano, Milan
t +39 02 48015069
www.cec-milano.com

Dedar, Appiano Gentile
t +39 031 228 7511
www.dedar.com

FABRICS – SOUTH AFRICA
African Sketchbook Fine Art
Fabrics, Cape Town
t +27 (0)21 715 6025
www.africansketchbook.com

Coral Stephens, Swaziland
t +26 (0)8437 1140
www.coralstephens.com

Homefabrics, Johannesburg
t +27 (0)11 266 3700
www.homefabrics.co.za

Mavromac, Johannesburg
t +27 (0)11 444 15854
info@mavromac.co.za

FABRICS – BANGKOK
Jim Thompson, The Thai Silk
Company Ltd, Bangkok
t +662 762 2600
www.jimthompson.com

**CURTAIN HARDWARE &
ACCESSORIES**
Barry London Glass
t +1 212 662 3370
www.barrylondonglass.com

The Bradley Collection
t +44 (0)845 118 7224 (Europe)
+1 310 815 8255 (USA)
www.bradleycollection.com

Fabricant
t +44 (0)845 688 0995
www.fabricant.co.uk

Jago Products Limited
t +44 (0)20 8810 5432
www.jagodesigns.co.uk

McKinney & Co.
t +44 (0)20 7627 5077
www.mckinney.co.uk

Palace Forge
t +1 404 266 9388

Silent Gliss Limited
t +44 (0)1843 863571
www.silentgliss.co.uk

Van Gregory & Norton
t +1 718 522 6546
www.vangregoryandnorton.com

READY-MADE CURTAINS
Blanc d'Ivoire
t +33 (0)1 45 44 41 17
www.blancdivoire.fr

Crate & Barrel
t +1 800 967 6696
www.crateandbarrel.com

Ethan Allen
t +1 888 eahelp1
www.ethanallen.com

IKEA
t +44 (0)8453 583 363 (UK)
+ 1 800 434-IKEA (USA)
www.ikea.com

John Lewis
t +44 08456 049 049
www.johnlewis.com

Martha Stewart
t +1 800 357 7060
www.marthastewart.com

West Elm
t +1 888 922 4119
www.westelm.com

Williams-Sonoma
t +1 877 812 6235
www.williams-sonoma.com

CURTAIN MAKERS
Bazzurro Designs
t +1 404 799 5674

Bay Tree Interiors
t +44 (0)1225 865744
www.amazingmaison.com

The Curtain Exchange
www.thecurtainexchange.co.uk

Doreen Scott
t +44 (0)1234 720975

Interiors Haberdashery
t +1 203 969 7227
www.interiorshaberdashery.com

Jane Clayton & Co.
t +44 (0)1761 412255
www.janeclayton.co.uk

Let It Loose
t +44 (0)1728 604700
www.thecottontree.co.uk

Margaret Sheridan
t +44 (0)1953 850691
www.margaretsheridan.co.uk

Steven Fabrics
t +1 800 328 2558
www.stevenfabrics.com

Willard Pitt
t +1 404 355 8232

DESIGNERS
John Barman Inc.
t +1 212 838 9443
www.johnbarman.com

Liz Biden
info@royalmalewane.com

Drake Design Associates
t +1 212 754 3099
www.drakedesignassociates.com

Luigi Esposito – Casa Forma
t +44 (0)7584 9495
www.casaforma.co.uk

Swatches

Boyd Fergusson
t: +27 21 425 5110

Tim Hobby – Space
t: +1 404 228 4600
www.spacemodern.com

Kelly Hoppen Interiors
t: +44 (0)20 7471 3350
www.kellyhoppen.com

Kit Kemp at Firmdale Hotels
t: +44 (0)20 7581 4045
www.firmdalehotels.com

Ralph Krall
t: +27 (0)21 424 6006
Shibumi4@mweb.co.za

Jacquelynne P Lanham Designs Inc.
t: +1 404 364 0472
www.lanhamdesigns.com

Larry Laslo – Larry Laslo Designs
t: +1 212 734 3824
www.larrylaslodesigns.com

Gizard Associés
t: +33 (0)1 55 28 38 58
www.gizardassocies.com

Hilton McConnico
t: +33 (0)143 625 316
www.hiltonmcconnico.com

Mimmi O'Connell
t: +44 (0)20 7752 0474
www.mimmioconnell.com

Mary-Bryan Peyer Designs Inc.
t: +1 912 638 0000
mbpeyer@bellsouth.net

Melanie Rademacher
t: +44 (0)7973 629 284
melanie@menainteriors.co.uk

Jonathan Reed – Studio Reed
t: +44 (0)20 7565 0066

Michael Tavano
t: +1 212 564 0034
www.michaeltavano.com

Jill Vantosh – Vantosh & Associates
t: +1 404 237 8686

Kathi Weixelbaumer
info@weixelbaumerdesign.co.za

Vicente Wolf Associates Inc.
t: +1 212 465 0590
www.vicentewolfassociates.com

Andrzej Zarzycki – Collett Zarzycki
t: +44 (0)20 8969 6967
www.collett-zarzycki.com

SHEERS
p.29: Istra Vanilla 7305/05, Romo.
p.30, left to right: Natures Web in Mica, Larry Laslo for Robert Allen; Narrow Stripe Pink Voile FCV720, Chelsea Textiles; Annabella Bianca 01 16459001, Fadini Borghi; Crinkle Bronze 3024, Roger Oates; Zanoli Opal 1151/11, Villa Nova; 8390-101, Kravet.

p.48: 1 Luxe Moonlight 3067, Harlequin; 2 Lina Quadra 41 Ivory, Nya Nordiska; 3 Shanti Zinc SHAN25, Malabar; 4 Angel DSSHAN301, Sanderson; 5 Inula Azure 7314/02, Romo; 6 Mul Mul 02 MULM02, Malabar; 7 Silhouette Natural RF7071/06, Romo; 8 Pesco 92156, Fadini Borghi; 9 Tela-Cross 67 Yellow, Nya Nordiska; 10 Ondollno 02 Beige; 11 Moustique 17101-003, Dominique Kieffer; 12 Thin Stripe Seamist Voile FCV715, Chelsea Textiles.
p.49, background: Ciliegio I92130, Fadini Borghi at Pierre Frey; top left: Shanti Ecru SHAN23 trimmed with Shanti Ashes SHAN20, Malabar; bottom left: Narrow Stripe Green Voile FCV718 trimmed with Green Linen, Chelsea Textiles; top right: Telá Lina 44 Peach, Nya Nordiska.

p.50 left to right: Sumptuous Pane in Cream 8618-1, Kravet; Many Facets in Kiwi, Larry Laslo for Robert Allen; Ricombo 32 Beige, Nya Nordiska; Dauncy Smoke, Robert Allen; Fareli Earth, Larry Laslo for Robert Allen.

p.62: 1 Grosgrain Sheer in Mint, Beacon Hill; 2 Buko 05 White/Red, Nya Nordiska; 3 Tela Baja 82 Black/White; 4 Opalin 2158-01, Sahco; 5 Dentelle de Coton Noir Vert de Gris 17109-001, Dominique Kieffer; 6 Orsino Check Pongee 8677-1, Kravet Couture; 7 Maille Lait 17143-001, Dominique Kieffer; 8 Woven Linen, Chelsea Textiles; 9 Voile Scattered Leaves and Sprigs F013, Chelsea Textiles; 10 Fleur de Lis, African Sketchbook; 11 Linen Truffle 8263-106, Kravet; 12 Freshness Marble, Larry Laslo for Robert Allen; 13 Ribbon Organza Amber 8920-6, Kravet Couture.
p.63, background: Indian Linen, Gold Book, Malabar; top left: Squiggle Embroidery on Silk 8424-106, edged with Silk Dupion, Kravet; top right: Timberland in Mica, by Larry Laslo for Robert Allen, edged in dark grey ribbon; Jasmin de Nuit 17080-001, Dominique Kieffer.

NATURALS
p.65: Pasha Ecru PASH23, Malabar.
p. 66, left to right: Pavilion Lime PV6, de Le Cuona; Congo Ebony CA7, de Le Cuona; Obi Linen 7150/03, Romo; Peasant Cloth Clay AA2, de Le Cuona; Antique Plain Linen Rose FAB2202, Roger Oates; Wind Sea Foam W15, de Le Cuona.

p.90: 1 Greystoke Cloud GRE5, de Le Cuona; 2 Kalina 09 Pink, Nya Nordiska; 3 Sprigs and Leaves in White on Green F199WG, Chelsea Textiles; 4 Pelham Stripe Aqua 9700-07, Blithfield & Co.; 5 Mailbag Canvas MA11, de Le Cuona; 6 Crepe de Lin Craie 17138-001, Dominique Kieffer; 7 Iroko Blanc 17094-001, Dominique Kieffer; 8 Lino 26 Cobalt, Nya Nordiska; 9 Rural Maple S1, de Le Cuona; 10 Issey Craie 17092-001, Dominique Kieffer; 11 Crepe de Lin Gris Bleu 17138-002, Dominique Kieffer.
p.91, background: Pasha Rice PASH26, Malabar; top left: Desert Cloth, Taupe BD8 and Soft Blue BD6, de Le Cuona; top right: Mali in Blue Ink, de Le Cuona; Grain of Rice 17137-001 by Dominique Kieffer.

p.92: 1 Leola Sesame RF7096/08, Romo; 2 Portfolio Steel PO1, de Le Cuona; 3 Dune Taupe AAA4, de Le Cuona; 4 Cape Dusk CP10, de Le Cuona; 5 Mummy's Cloth 7950 01 Currant, Donghia; 6 Thunder Swamp TH3, de Le Cuona; 7 Tozan Bleu Brun 17071-003, Dominique Kieffer; 8 Bundu Stripe Mint BS4, de Le Cuona; 9 Moleskin Plum 4109, Roger Oates; 10 Cluny Jacquard, Chelsea Textiles.
p.93, background: Skye Linen F5680-09, Osborne & Little; top left: Tailleur Check LF4421-06, Liberty, edged with Skye Linen FS680/02, Osborne & Little; bottom left: Karoo Soft Stone KAR2, de Le Cuona; right: Jackdaw Steel JAC2, de Le Cuona.

GLAMOUR
p.94: Siam 40, Malabar.
p.96, left to right: Petite Ribbons Toast Multi, Beacon Hill; Amaya TA03 Wine, Pongees; Alexei Putty, Andrew Martin; Riley Stripe in Aqua F3418/04, Colefax & Fowler; Sonate Rouge, Manuel Canovas; Chinchilla Clove, de Le Cuona.

p.120: 1 Lineas Amethyst, Beacon Hill; 2 Taffetas Fontages Shot Pink, Claremont; 3 Hana TA01 0163 Lichen, Pongees; 4 Lyric Linden DLYRLY303, Sanderson; 5 Simple Star in Driftwood, Larry Laslo for Robert Allen; 6 Capri Stripe in Ice Blue/Flax/Ebony 3315, J Robert Scott; 7 Global Silk BL6631/5 DGRIGB307, Sanderson; 8 Moonga Peek-A-Boo MOON19, Malabar; 9 Cing Mers Rust Bronze, Claremont;

10 Rivington HX02 0233 Putty, Pongees; 11 Barberini Burnt Apricot and Silvery Gold, Claremont; 12 Taffetas Plissé Pourpre 17058-9, Dominique Kieffer.
p.121, background: Siam 38, Malabar; top left: Mordoré 17107-011, Dominique Kieffer; top right: Pallisy HX06 0030 Berry, edged in Indian Douppion Fuschia 745/0125, Pongees; bottom: Sonate 4630/02, Manuel Canovas.

p.122: 1 Alexei Anenome, Andrew Martin; 2 Congress Sandcastle, Andrew Martin; 3 Silk Velvet Royal Yellow, de Le Cuona; 4 Orsello Ebony 7159/01, Romo; 5 Washington Velvet in Cornflower 323, Andrew Martin; 6 Rousillion Elderberry 7158/07, Romo; 7 New Manor Park PB39 044, Blendworth; 8 Satin 22261, Ulf Moritz for Sahco; 9 Verdant Pumice, Larry Laslo for Robert Allen; 10 Argonne Cut Velvet Golden 4438, J Robert Scott; 11 Strata 1879-03, Sahco Hesslein; 12 Damas Kaki 17116-004, Dominique Kieffer.
p.123, background: Palazzo Jute RF7136/60, Romo; top left: Silk Velvet in Pewter, lined with Mistral in Grape, de Le Cuona; bottom left: Palazzo Praline RF7136/47, Romo.

WOOL
p.124: Cha Cha Weaves Quickstep NCF3570/01, Nina Campbell.
p.125, left to right: Blackberry Mohair, Coral Stephens; Crescendo Damask, Mulberry; Cashmere Watermark Fawn, de Le Cuona; Wool Satin Spring FD562 Y103, Mulberry; London Check FD542, Mulberry; Hornbuckle Red Earth NNN5, de Le Cuona.

p.138: 1 Antique Paisley Blue U3, de Le Cuona; 2 Ethereal Silver ED85053, G P & J Baker; 3 Waverley Plaid Red/Bronze FD582 M13, Mulberry; 4 Hush Dove ED85052, G P & J Baker; 5 Odyssey Ebony 4006/08, Kirkby House; 6 Whistler Fig ED85041 580, G P & J Baker; 7 Minim Chocolate FD612 A120, Mulberry; 8 Quaver Check Sage FD613 S108, Mulberry; 9 Bandit Blue TA2, de Le Cuona; 10 Mulberry Wool Satin Pear FD562 S27, Mulberry; 11 Southwark Ebony, Andrew Martin.
p.139, background: Ethereal Champagne ED85053, G P & J Baker; top: 100 per cent mohair, hand-dyed, Coral Stephens; bottom left: Faded Stripe FD544-W28, Mulberry, bordered with Moleskin Plum 4109, Roger Oates; bottom right: Buttermilk Wool Satin FD562 T45, Mulberry.

PATTERNS
p.141: Greystoke Natural GRE2, de Le Cuona.
p.142, left to right: Griffin Green/Natural 9900/02, Blithfield & Co.; Small check with Accent Mauve FC475, Chelsea Textiles; Gilby Cranberry 7234/15, Romo; Wickham Apple 7223/31, Romo; Maris Watermelon 7262/02, Romo; Milford Indigo 7231/13, Romo.

p.154: 1 Generous Rosewood, Larry Laslo for Robert Allen; 2 Ticking in Almond and Khaki FT950, Chelsea Textiles; 3 Small Check Raspberry FC453, Chelsea Textiles; 4 Indian Silk – Ebony Book NSIL03, Malabar; 5 Kobana Stripe NCF3802/05, Nina Campbell; 6 Large Accent Check in Almond and Chestnut FCA205, Chelsea Textiles; 7 Blue Check, Cabbages & Roses; 8 Tyneham Apple 7224/31, Romo; 9 Square Dance NCF3571/02, Nina Campbell.
p.155, background: Oska 13, Malabar; top left: Petits Carreaux Bleu Jean 17139-008, Dominique Kieffer; bottom left: Mini Check Blue FC605A and Wide Stripe Seafoam FT560, Chelsea Textiles; right: Duoline Stripe 2002 Blue, edged with Moleskin Blue, Roger Oates.

p.156: left to right: India Rose, Cabbages & Roses; Brocante Rose Indigo on Natural, Brocante; Abbey Dore 01, Elanbach; French Toile in Raspberry, Cabbages & Roses; French Floral Stone, FL13, Elanbach.

p.172: 1 Parnham blue/green 5400-03, Blithfield & Co.; 2 Temple Garden Beaches 173582, Jamie Drake for Schumacher; 3 Tulip & Roses, Cabbages & Roses; 4 Vincent Citrus ZWAT04004, Zoffany; 5 Cow Parsley CP16/8, Vanessa Arbuthnott; 6 Hay Bluff 04 Stone, Elanbach; 7 Opera Rose, African Sketchbook.
p.173, background: Blue Natural Hatley, Cabbages & Roses; top left: No. 9 Jim's Garden 2042/02, Jim Thompson; below left: Elizabeth Sage, Ernest & Matlida, edged with Alaska 90 F0530870/133, Crowson; below: Lavande Natural, Brocante, edged with Skye Linen F5680-09, Osborne & Little.

HARDWARE
p.180: Elsa Oro 045 16473004, Fadini Borghi.

Index

Acknowledgements

No book of this character, that breaks new ground and explores new and exciting visions and designs, can be produced without an enormous amount of hard work and generosity from a great number of people in the design industry. So many of my friends and colleagues have given their time, ideas, fabrics and contacts that I feel humbled. I know that without them, I would not have been able to produce a book of this quality and with so many wonderful and original ideas. Thank you so much one and all.

Bernie de Le Cuona, a visionary designer of fabrics and a treasured friend, gave unstintingly of her advice, fabrics and ideas. It was while listening to her and watching the way in which she combined fabrics and simple style that I realized that the crux of the book really was 'let the fabrics do the talking'.

Dominique Kieffer, another quite extraordinary fabric designer – this time from Paris – let us photograph her apartment as well as experiment with her totally unique and exciting fabrics. We were also introduced to her charming daughter and allowed to photograph her divine 'shoebox' apartment. Meeting them both has been a real treat.

Larry Laslo, his fabulous colleague Bonnie Steves and the wonderful Jolie Cross Cohen at The Robert Allen Group all made so much happen for us in New York, in order that we could photograph Larry's new and innovative collection of sheers in his marvellous Manhattan home. Talk about moving mountains!

Vicente Wolf and his great team, who gave us access to two great Manhattan apartments to photograph for the book. As ever, his work is an inspiration and adds lustre to any book I write. His clients welcomed us and helped us with information and coffee in the most hospitable way.

Jackye Lanham was, as always, a pillar of strength, not to mention loads of fun and friendship in Atlanta, but this time she went the extra mile for us and flew down to Jacksonville so that we could photograph her dream home on the beach at Punta Verde, as well as several other homes nearby. It was wonderful to be entertained in her perfect beach home and to be treated to lovely meals there. She makes decorating look effortless and everything else great fun. Thanks also to Jackye's team, and to Natalie Evans of Low Country Luxe, who organized Sea Island for us and the lovely home designed by Mary-Bryan Peyer for us to shoot.

The adorable Jennifer Brady, as always, looked after us, found us houses to shoot and the best place in Atlanta to buy lunch! An enormous thank you is due to her, especially for finding us the house designed by Jill Vantosh.

Tim Hobby, again for finding us houses to shoot and for always being such an inspiration. We were photographing at Space, his downtown business, right up to the point when we left Atlanta.

Mimmi O'Connell, who let us photograph her London home, and Gonzales, who made us the best lunch. Mimmi was, as ever, inspiring, and her home was quite perfect.

Luigi Esposito was of enormous assistance to us, as he has always been before, and we were delighted to photograph the stunning apartment in London that he had designed for a client in his oh-so elegant way.

Kit Kemp's marvellously original style for the Haymarket Hotel in London was exciting and fulfilling for us all. Our special thanks also to Craig Markham, for making so many rooms available to us – we know how difficult that is in a busy hotel (www.firmdale.com).

Andrzej Zarzycki, who worked with us when we photographed the beautiful home in London which he had designed for his clients, and who explained everything so well.

Di and Ann from African Sketchbook in Cape Town turned themselves into whirling dervishes to make sure that we photographed as many different fabrics in as many different places as possible. They were the only people who actually made a pair of curtains in front of my eyes as the camera was rolling.

Everyone at the Cape Grace Hotel in Cape Town (www.capegrace.com), who let us photograph the rooms designed by Kathi Weixelbaumer, reworking and reinventing this wonderful hotel into something not only totally different, but also quite stunning. We were finishing as the first guests were arriving.

Liz Biden found time for us to photograph all the exquisite suites at La Residence in Franschhoek (www.laresidence.co.za), one of the most beautiful areas of South Africa, if not the world. There I found the silk curtains in vibrant colours that I had been dreaming about and which added an element of glamour and verve to my book. Thank you, also, to Len, Johan and all the staff at La Residence for a delicious lunch and loads of help.

There are so many people that in one way or another were of enormous assistance in this project – Sue Smirron and the team at Coral Stephens in Swaziland; Claire, Kathi and everyone at Bishopsgrace Hotel in Cape Town (www.bishopsgrace.com); Roger Oates, Jonathan Reed, Christina Strutt of Cabbages & Roses and Mona Perlhagen of Chelsea Textiles in the UK; John Barman in New York; Mary-Bryan Peyer in Atlanta; and Hilton McConnico and Stephanie Schlemmer in Paris.

A huge thank you to Zia Mattocks, whose calm patience is a huge plus for me, and Alison Davidson, who helped me with so much of the source material – I could not have coped without them.

Also thank you to Simon Upton for his wonderful photography in Europe and the USA, and Greg Cox for his photography in South Africa. And to Nadine Bazar for location research and Sarah Rock for her stylish design.

Lastly, to Jacqui Small from whom I learn more with each book we do together and who lets me go places and do things in my own special way – thank you.

Picture credits

All photographs by Simon Upton unless otherwise stated:

1 Jacquelynne Lanham's house in Florida; **2–3** a house in Atlanta, designed by Tim Hobby of Space; **4** a New York town house designed by Larry Laslo for LL Designs; **5** designer Kelly Hoppen/Vincent Knapp; **6 left** Eric Gizard Associés/Christophe Fillioux; **7** La Residence, Franschhoek designed by Liz Biden/Greg Cox; **8 left** La Residence, Franschhoek designed by Liz Biden/Greg Cox; **8 right** Hilton McConnico's home in Paris; **9** La Residence, Franschhoek designed by Liz Biden/Greg Cox; **10 left** Bernie de la Cuona; **14–15** a house in Georgia designed by Jacquelynne P Lanham Designs Inc.; **16 below** Jacquelynne Lanham's house in Florida; **17** a house in London designed by Melanie Rademacher; **18 above** Roger & Fay Oates's house in Herefordshire; **18 below** Dominique Kieffer's apartment in Paris; **18 right** Hilton McConnico's home in Paris; **19** a house in Atlanta, designed by Jill Vantosh/Vantosh & Associates; **20 above** John Barman's apartment in New York; **21 above left** a house in London, designed by Melanie Rademacher; **21 above right** a house in Georgia, designed by Jacquelynne P Lanham Designs Inc.; **21 below** an apartment in Paris, designed by Hilton McConnico; **22 above left** Fazia Seth of Casa Forma's London apartment; **22 below left** a house in Georgia, designed by Jacquelynne P Lanham Designs Inc.; **23** a cottage on Sea Island, designed by Mary-Bryan Peyer Designs Inc.; **24 above left** designer Kelly Hoppen/Vincent Knapp; **24 above right** designed by Stephen Sills and James Huniford/Ken Hayden; **25 left** Stephanie Hoppen's apartment in London; **25 above right** designer Kelly Hoppen/Vincent Knapp; **26** Stephanie Hoppen's apartment in London; **27 above right** designer Kelly Hoppen/Vincent Knapp; **27 below right** a Park Avenue apartment, designed by Vicente Wolf; **28–9** a house in Atlanta, designed by Jill Vantosh/Vantosh & Associates; **31–3** a house in Atlanta, designed by Tim Hobby of Space; **34** Dominique Kieffer's apartment in Paris; **36–7** a house in Atlanta, designed by Jill Vantosh/Vantosh & Associates; **38–9** Jacquelynne Lanham's house in Florida; **40** a house in Georgia, designed by Jacquelynne P Lanham Designs Inc.; **41** an apartment in New York, designed by Vicente Wolf; **42** a house in Florida, designed by Jacquelynne P Lanham Designs Inc.; **43 above** a Park Avenue apartment, designed by Vicente Wolf; **43 below** Stephanie Hoppen's apartment in London; **44–5** an apartment in New York, designed by Vicente Wolf; **46–7** an apartment in Paris, designed by Hilton McConnico; **51–3** a New York town house designed by Larry Laslo for LL Designs; **55** Bishopsgrace in Cape Town, designed by Kathi Weixelbaumer/Greg Cox; **56–7** a cottage on Sea Island designed by Mary-Bryan Peyer Designs Inc.; **58–9** a Kips Bay apartment designed by Larry Laslo for LL Designs; **60** a New York town house designed by Larry Laslo for LL Designs; **61 below** Jacquelynne Lanham's house in Atlanta; **64–5** Dominique Kieffer's apartment in Paris; **67** Christina Strutt of Cabbages & Roses' house in Gloucestershire; **68** a house in London designed by Collett Zarzycki; **69** Dominique Kieffer's apartment in Paris; **70–1** Jacquelynne Lanham's house in Florida; **72** a house in Florida designed by Jacquelynne P Lanham Designs Inc.; **74–5** Mimmi O'Connell's house in London; **76** Cape Grace in Cape Town, designed by Kathi Weixelbaumer/Greg Cox; **77** an apartment in Paris, designed by Hilton McConnico; **78 above** a house in Florida, designed by Jacquelynne P Lanham Designs Inc.; **79** Jacquelynne Lanham's house in Florida; **80–1** Dominique Kieffer's apartment in Paris; **82 above** John Barman's apartment in New York; **82 below** an apartment in New York, designed by Drake Design Associates; **83** Cape Grace in Cape Town, designed by Kathi Weixelbaumer/Greg Cox; **84–5** Charlotte de la Grandière's apartment in Paris, with fabrics by Dominique Kieffer; **86 below** designer Kelly Hoppen/Vincent Knapp; **87** a house in Florida, designed by Jacquelynne P Lanham Designs Inc.; **88–9** The Haymarket Hotel, designed by Kit Kemp; **94–5** a house in London designed by Collett Zarzycki; **97** Carey & Doug Benham's house in Atlanta; **98–9** Fazia Seth of Casa Forma's London apartment; **100 left** La Residence, Franschhoek designed by Liz Biden/Greg Cox; house in Atlanta; **102–4** a house in Atlanta, designed by Jill Vantosh/Vantosh & Associates; **105** Mimmi O'Connell's house in London; **106 left** La Residence, Franschhoek designed by Liz Biden/Greg Cox; **106 right** Hilton McConnico's home in Paris; **107** Cape Grace in Cape Town, designed by Kathi Weixelbaumer/Greg Cox; **108–9** a house in London designed by Melanie Rademacher; **110–11** Stephanie Hoppen's apartment in London; **112 left** a house in Atlanta, designed by Hank Hitopolous; **112 right** La Residence, Franschhoek designed by Liz Biden/Greg Cox; **113** La Residence, Franschhoek designed by Liz Biden/Greg Cox; **114–15** Fazia Seth of Casa Forma's London apartment; **116 above** a house in London designed by Collett Zarzycki; **117** designed by Casa Forma/© Chris Tubbs; **118–19** Dominique Kieffer's apartment in Paris; **124–25** a house in Atlanta designed by Tim Hobby of Space; **127** a house in Atlanta, designed by Hank Hitopolous; **128–9** Jacquelynne Lanham's house in Atlanta; **130** a house in London designed by Collett Zarzycki; **131 right** designed by Casa Forma/© Chris Tubbs; **132–3** a house in London designed by Collett Zarzycki; **134–5** a house in Atlanta, designed by Hank Hitopolous; **136–7** a New York town house designed by Larry Laslo for LL Designs; **140–3** The Haymarket Hotel, designed by Kit Kemp; **144** Roger & Fay Oates's house in Herefordshire; **145** a house in Georgia designed by Jacquelynne P Lanham Designs Inc.; **146** a New York town house designed by Larry Laslo for LL Designs; **147** a Kips Bay apartment designed by Larry Laslo for LL Designs; **148** The Haymarket Hotel, designed by Kit Kemp; **149 above** designed by Drake Design Associates/© Lucas Allen; **149 below** Roger & Fay Oates's house in Herefordshire; **150** a house in London, designed by Jonathan Reed; **151** Bishopsgrace in Cape Town, designed by Kathi Weixelbaumer/Greg Cox; **152–3** a house in Georgia designed by Jacquelynne P Lanham Designs Inc.; **157** The Haymarket Hotel, designed by Kit Kemp; **158 above** Mr & Mrs Sagbakken's cabin by the sea (Norway), interior design by Helene Forbes-Hennis; **159** a house in Georgia designed by Jacquelynne P Lanham Designs Inc.; **160 & 161 below left** an apartment at The Apthorp in New York City; **161 right–163** Christina Strutt of Cabbages & Roses' house in Gloucestershire; **164–5** The Haymarket Hotel, designed by Kit Kemp; **166** a house in Georgia designed by Jacquelynne P Lanham Designs Inc.; **167** a house in London designed by Jonathan Reed; **168** Hout Bay Manor designed by Boyd Ferguson of Cécile & Boyd's/Greg Cox; **169** Cape Grace in Cape Town, designed by Kathi Weixelbaumer/Greg Cox; **170–1** Jacquelynne Lanham's house in Florida; **174** a house in Atlanta, designed by Tim Hobby of Space; **176–7** John Barman's apartment in New York; **178** Mimmi O'Connell's house in London; **179 above & below left** a house in Atlanta, designed by Tim Hobby of Space; **179 below right** a house in London designed by Jonathan Reed; **181** Mimmi O'Connell's house in London; **182** Silent Gliss Limited; **183** Bishopsgrace in Cape Town, designed by Kathi Weixelbaumer/Greg Cox; **184 above left** The Bradley Collection; **185 above right & below** Fabricant Limited; **185** Van Gregory & Norton; **186** Jago Products Limited; **187 above left** The Bradley Collection.